INSIGHT
EXPL

NEW YORK

CONTENTS

ART ENTHUSIASTS

There's more art than can be seen in a lifetime: from the big five – the Met (route 6), MoMA (route 3), Whitney, Guggenheim, and Frick (route 7) – to Chelsea's gallery scene (route 11).

RECOMMENDED ROUTES FOR...

NIGHTLIFE

Check out the alt-rock scene on the Lower East Side (route 14); catch a set at a Greenwich Village jazz club (route 12) or Harlem's Apollo (route 9); or dance all night at a Meatpacking District hotspot (route 12).

MOVIE BUFFS' NEW YORK

King Kong clambered up the Empire State Building (route 1); Holly Golightly breakfasted at Tiffany's (walk 1); Travis Bickle wandered Times Square (route 2); and the Corleones caused big trouble in Little Italy (route 14).

FOODIES

For fresh produce try Union Square Greenmarket, Eataly or Chelsea Market (route 11), while Dean & Deluca (route 13) and Katz's Delicatessen (route 14) are packed with gourmet goodies.

THE PERFORMING ARTS

Take in a Broadway show on the Great White Way (route 2); the ballet at Lincoln Center (route 8); an off-Broadway romp in the East Village (route 14); or free Shakespeare in Central Park (route 5).

SHOPPERS

Go on a shopping spree at Fifth Avenue department stores (route 1); visit boutiques in Soho (route 13) and the Meatpacking District (route 12); or browse 18 miles of books at the Strand Book Store (route 12).

SKYSCRAPER SPOTTING

Explore the vertical city, including the Flatiron (route 11), the Art Deco-era Chrysler (route 4), and Empire State (route 1), and high-rise Lower Manhattan (route 15).

SPECTACULAR VIEWS

Take in glorious views from the Empire State Building (route 1), Top of the Rock at Rockefeller Center (route 1), Brooklyn Bridge (route 17), Statue of Liberty (route 16), or Staten Island Ferry (route 16).

INTRODUCTION

An introduction to New York's geography, customs and culture, plus illuminating background information on cuisine, history and what to do when you're there.

Fifth Avenue at night

EXPLORE NEW YORK

The 50 million-plus visitors who come each year arrive with skyscraper-high expectations, but with jaw-dropping architecture, world-class cultural sights, and fabulous shops and restaurants, the Big Apple does not disappoint.

In his writings on the city, *Here is New York*, the children's author, critic, and Pulitzer Prize-winner E.B. White wrote, 'New York is nothing like Paris; it is nothing like London; and it is not Spokane multiplied by sixty, or Detroit multiplied by four. It is by all odds the loftiest of cities. It even managed to reach the highest point in the sky at the lowest moment of the Depression.'

Since its purchase by the Dutch in 1626, through its growth as a maritime hub, to its contemporary position as the cultural and financial center of the United States, New York his risen to become a crossroads of the world and a place where the air tingles with the promise that everything is possible.

Statistics

The statistics are quite something: 6,400 miles (10,300km) of streets, 578 miles (930km) of waterfront, 18,000 restaurants, around 13,000 taxis, over 6,000 city buses, 150 museums, and 400 art galleries, more than 240 theaters, and 29,000 acres (11,736 hectares) of parks. Whatever you're after, from world-class museums on the Upper East Side to cutting-edge couture in the Meatpacking District, you'll find it here. If you stay in a sky-high hotel far above the teeming streets, or stroll in Central Park, or walk out onto the terrace overlooking the Hudson River at the Cloisters, you may even be able to find that city-center rarity: peace and quiet.

Posing on the Brooklyn Bridge

THE BOROUGHS

New York City covers a surface area of 301 sq miles (780 sq km), and is

Statue of Liberty   *Downtown Manhattan from the Brooklyn Bridge*

divided into five boroughs: Manhattan, Brooklyn, Queens, the Bronx, and Staten Island. Manhattan, which is the smallest borough, has a surface area of almost 24 sq miles (62 sq km), but is also the most densely populated part of the city.

It remains open to debate how New York got its 'Big Apple' tag. Some say that the nickname came from a 1920s newspaper column about horse racing called 'Around the Big Apple.' Others say it was used by jazz players to indicate getting to the top of their profession, or reaching 'the Big Apple.'

NEW YORKERS

Population and melting pot

According to the US Census Bureau, New York City has a population of 8.2 million. Of that figure, approximately 1.6 million people reside in Manhattan, 2.6 million in Brooklyn, 2.3 million in Queens, 1.4 million in the Bronx, and around 470,000 in Staten Island.

Although there are other cities in the United States with a high percentage of foreign-born residents, none can match the range or diversity of the ethnic communities of New York. Here, around 33 percent of inhabitants are of European descent, 23 percent are African-American or African-Caribbean, 29 percent are Hispanic, and 13 percent are Asian. A former mayor, David Dinkins, once described the city as a 'gorgeous mosaic.'

The classic New Yorker

New Yorkers are stereotypically portrayed as being as relentlessly energetic as their home town is fast-paced. Frenetic or not (recent polls have shown that New York is not quite as super-speedy as its reputation might suggest – a 2007 survey of urban walking speeds put New Yorkers in only eighth place, after Singapore and Copenhagen), this energy is perhaps what gives New Yorkers their edge and makes them so sure that Manhattan is the center of the universe. Increasing numbers are choosing to retire in the city, lured by the ease of getting around and the many attractions.

Resilience is also a key attribute. The reaction of most city inhabitants to the attacks of September 11, 2001, when terrorists crashed two hijacked jets into the towering World Trade Center, or more recently when Hurricane Sandy caused havoc in Lower Manhattan, was to respond with characteristic resolve to recover and rebuild.

CLIMATE

New York is blessed with sunshine year-round, but it has four distinct seasons. Summers can be steamy, with temperatures as high as 96°F (36°C), and winter days may dip as low as 10°F (-12°C). Happily, extreme heat or cold spells are usually brief; typical summer day temperatures are around 85°F (29°C) and winters in the 30–45°F

Greenwich's White Horse Tavern

(-1–7°C) range. Snowfalls are generally light, though every few years a major storm blankets the city, which thrills cross-country skiers, who head for Central Park. April brings showers, but May and June can be delightful, and the bright fall weather in September and October makes this the ideal time to visit. Spring and fall days average 60–75°F (15–24°C).

WATERWAYS

New York lies at the mouth of the Hudson River, which borders Manhattan's West Side. On the other side, the East River, separating Manhattan from Brooklyn and Queens, is a narrow strip of water linking Long Island Sound and Upper New York Bay. The southern portions of Brooklyn and Queens have sandy shores on the Atlantic Ocean. It is estimated that it takes strong swimmers an average of seven hours and 15 minutes to swim around Manhattan (not recommended).

A WALKERS' CITY

Unlike many cities in the United States, New York is a great place for walkers, helped by the fact that for the most part it is organized on a straightforward grid plan – numbered streets (north–south) and avenues (east–west). Pay little heed to the fancied-up Avenue of the Americas tag for good old Sixth Avenue, but watch out for the crazy-quilt pattern below 14th Street.

The West Village has streets unique to its neighborhood, many running at odd angles, which makes navigating this area a fun challenge even for long-time New Yorkers. Things really change south of Houston Street, where the numbered streets end altogether. Keep in mind that Fifth Avenue and, to the north, Central Park, mark the division between east and west.

Staying safe

Some people fear walking around New York because of supposed pick-pockets or would-be attackers, but in fact the city has been one of America's safest large cities for years. Such crime that

---

Urban woodland

When Henry Hudson sailed up the river that bears his name, his first mate, Robert Juett, wrote: 'We found a land full of great tall oaks, with grass and flowers, as pleasant as ever has been seen.' New York still has over 28,000 acres (11,300 hectares) of parks, of which 10,000 acres (4,000 hectares) are wooded. Peregrine falcons nest on Midtown skyscraper ledges, and coyotes occasionally prowl from Westchester County down into the Bronx. Frederick Law Olmsted, the architect who laid out Central Park, wrote that, 'the contemplation of natural scenes… is favorable to the health and vigor of men.'

Busy streets   *In Little Italy*

does occur tends to be as random in nature as absolutely anywhere else in the world, and, as elsewhere, ostentatious displays of jewelry or wealth tend to invite unwanted attention.

Since New York is generally a lively place at all hours, there are only a few locations you should avoid. Most streets are consistently populated – although Midtown and southern Manhattan business areas are more deserted in the evenings, when the East and West Villages and Theatre District are hopping. Central Park, Battery Park, and Harlem are best avoided after dark.

DON'T LEAVE NEW YORK WITHOUT...

Taking in a view of the city skyline. Whether you ascend the Empire State Building for a panoramic view, lie back in Central Park looking up at the forest of buildings, or cross the Brooklyn Bridge for an unimpeded look at Lower Manhattan's skyline, be sure to find a place to survey what is possibly the world's greatest urban landscape. See page 26, page 46, and page 96.

Sailing to see the Statue of Liberty. Hop aboard a direct ferry (which also goes on to Ellis Island) or grab a free ride on the Staten Island Ferry to bag yourself a prime view of Lady Liberty. See page 95.

Paying a visit to MoMa. With one of the most incredible collections of modern art in the world, including works by Picasso, Hopper, and Van Gogh, housed in a purpose-built gallery that is noteworthy in and of itself, MoMa is unmissable. See page 36.

A walk along the High Line. Climb one of its many entrance stairways to quickly escape the hurried crowds and metallic roars of the city. The path, lined with native flora and wooden benches, is ideal for wiling away an hour or for a relaxed stroll between Chelsea and the Meatpacking District. See page 80.

Stocking up on local eats. Visit local institution Zabar's, in the Upper West Side, chow down on a streetside hot dog, or explore the Lower East Side's range of traditional Jewish foods. See page 62 and page 88.

Giving your regards to Broadway. Even if you can't get tickets to a show, spend some time among the bright lights of the Great White Way, perhaps stopping for a deli lunch amidst portraits of famous theatrical folk. See page 32.

Crossing the Brooklyn Bridge. Marvel at the incredible 19th-century engineering as you cross this iconic bridge, which leads to the ever-increasingly hip borough of Brooklyn. See page 96.

Getting out at night. Whether it's listening to jazz in a classic Greenwich joint or supping cocktails in an achingly hip Meatpacking District bar, find out why New York has a reputation as the city that never sleeps. See page 122.

Times Square draws in the crowds

SUBWAYS, BUSES AND TAXIS

In addition to the city being so straight-forward to navigate on foot, it also has excellent subway and bus systems. You can sometimes find paper maps at sub-way stations and on buses, but there are also excellent transportation apps for most smart phones. Despite reports to the contrary, subways are consid-ered fairly clean and safe – although it's still best to avoid traveling on your own after 11pm. The subway is usually the fastest way of getting around, espe-cially for long distances, although walk-ing is generally quicker if you're only traveling a few blocks.

Buses are useful and, while very slow, may seem less intimidating than

Cabs are ever present on New York streets

navigating the subway. They are best for traveling cross-town (east-west) and can be a cheap way to see the sights. Each bus has a digital destina-tion sign, and route maps are posted at every stop.

Those iconic yellow taxis are easy to become dependent on – unlike many cities, where you have to arrange for taxis in advance, in New York they just seem to appear (except when it's rain-ing) and can be hailed anywhere you spot the light signifying the cab is avail-able. New York taxis date from 1907, when John Hertz founded the Yellow Cab Company. He chose this color after reading a study that said that yel-low was the easiest to spot. Cab fares can mount up fast. Note that if you're trying to get somewhere at rush hour, it can be a long, frustrating, and expen-sive ride, and it's probably a better idea to catch the subway.

An exceptional city

By the end of their first trip to New York, most visitors are hooked. Noth-ing is quite as exhilarating as walking between the skyscrapers of Midtown for the first time, or seeing the iconic Statue of Liberty looming over you from the ferry dock. Or even just strolling through Central Park on a sunny day or a blustery winter afternoon. Remem-ber to walk purposefully and you'll fit right in. You'll soon discover why New Yorkers have a right to feel that there's no place quite like their home.

Classic souvenirs for sale

TOP TIPS FOR EXPLORING NEW YORK

Reservations. Unless you plan to eat at a diner or cafeteria, be sure to call ahead to book, especially for hot new spots. And even if you have 'resos,' don't be surprised if you still have to wait a while to be seated. The only surefire way of beating the crowds is to eat at off-hours.

Apple Store. You can surf the web and check your email (for free!) at New York's flagship Apple Store on any one of the computers on display 24 hours a day, 365 days a year.

Cheap tickets. Discount tickets for same-day shows can be purchased at the TKTS booth on Duffy Square. Evening tickets: Mon–Sat 3–8pm, Tue 2–8pm, Sun 3pm–30 mins before curtain; matinee tickets: Wed, Sat 10am–2pm, Sun 11am–3pm; cash or travelers checks only.

Joint tickets and talks. Joint tickets are available for access to both MoMA and Top of the Rock, saving 20 percent off the cost of two single tickets. Free gallery talks at MoMA are offered daily at 11.30am and 1.30pm. Family tours and workshops are available, too, with programs designed especially for children.

Bike lane. Upper-West-siders can now go faster (and safer) by bike with the bike lane on Columbus Avenue that stretches from 96th to 77th street. In 2013, the city approved plans to extend the lane south to 59th and north 110th street. Alternatively, cycle through Central Park – park roads are closed to traffic on weekends. Rentals are available at 348 West 57th Street, near Ninth Avenue, tel: 212-664-9600; www.bikerentalcentralpark.com.

Harlem guided tours. Harlem Spirituals (tel: 212-391-0900; www.harlemspirituals.com) and Harlem Heritage Tours (tel: 212-280-7888; www.harlemheritage.com) offer some of the best guided tours in the district, with themes such as heritage and history, gospel on Sundays, and evening jazz excursions.

Medieval music. Call 212-650-2290 for information about concerts at The Cloisters. Performances are held in the 12th-century Fuentidueña Chapel and feature medieval compositions played on period instruments. Concert ticket prices include free same-day admission to the museum.

Governors Island. Once a major US military base, this is now 172 acres (70 hectares) of parkland offering walking and biking trails, historic forts and buildings, picnicking and peerless views. Free 10-minute ferry rides from the Maritime Terminal near Battery Park Sat–Sun 10am–7pm from June–October (www.govisland.com).

Long Island beaches. Although New York lies on the coast, the beaches accessible by subway tend to be crowded, especially on hot summer weekends. The nicest are two to three hours by train or bus from Manhattan, on Long Island or in New Jersey.

Striped bass at Daniel

FOOD AND DRINK

Visitors will quickly discover why New Yorkers are passionate about food. The city boasts an amazing variety of delicious choices, haute cuisine to street carts, with prices to match.

New York has always had a reputation as a culinary melting pot. From Jewish delicatessens to Mexican taco joints to a vast market full of Italian eateries, people can enjoy a staggering range of food at every price point – they can order a $2 hot dog or a $32 hamburger. Diners are a New York institution found in almost every neighborhood, serving from breakfast through dinner with a wide variety of choices from snacks, sandwiches, and salads to full meals, all at moderate prices. The city's top-drawer restaurants take pride in serving the very best of French, Italian, Asian and New American cuisine.

FASHIONS IN FOOD

Fashions are vital in New York, and the contemporary fashion is for famous-name kitchens fronted by celebrity chefs, both homegrown and from as far afield as London, Paris, and Italy. Current stars include Jean-Georges Vongerichten, David Chang, and April Bloomfield.

Another current fashion is to preface food styles by the words 'haute' and 'real,' stressing quality and authenticity. 'Haute Italian' describes Italian cuisine at its most elaborate, for example. Menus that change with the seasons, stressing foods fresh from local farms, are points of pride for many restaurants, as are organically grown vegetables and preservative-free meats and poultry.

Special diets

While 'vegetarian' has graduated from a regular option to a mainstay, with vegan choices increasingly available, the extreme theme is continued with diets containing the prefix 'free' ('dairy-free' or 'gluten-free,' for example). These terms are sprinkled over menus in New York, making it possible for everyone to find suitable food, whatever their dietary requirements.

FOOD SHOPS

Vital to New York's food culture are gourmet shops, delicatessens, and bakeries. At the high end are Zabar's, Dean & Deluca, Eataly, and Barney Greengrass, which carry premium meats, fish, cheeses, baked goods, and

Trendy Balthazar

prepared foods. More modest in size (but not quality) are mom-and-pop ethnic stores: traditional Italian and Jewish delicatessens, bagel shops, pastry shops, and Asian markets.

TRENDS BY AREA

Midtown

Some of the world's finest and most expensive restaurants – the Four Seasons, Le Bernadin, and Per Se to name but a few – are located in Midtown. Many Manhattan mainstays are here too, with the longevity prize going to the fabulous centenarian Oyster Bar at Grand Central Terminal.

For Midtown dining, it pays to do your homework. While spontaneity is fun farther downtown, in Midtown it's best to make reservations, especially to dine before or after the theater.

Restaurants here, especially the more expensive ones, often have formal dress codes. Men are suited (or at least jacketed) and women go groomed for a glamorous night on the town. Many Midtown restaurants are closed Sundays, and for lunch on Saturdays, as their corporate customers have gone.

Meatpacking District, Chelsea, Soho, and Tribeca

The Meatpacking District is good for both dining and posing, even if the patrons are often wafer-thin models who look as if they never eat. Chelsea Market, at Ninth Avenue and 15th Street, is heaven for food fetishists – a dozen or so bakeries, meat markets, kitchen suppliers, and other stores of a gastronomic bent, along with trendy dining places.

Once Soho gained recognition as an artistic center, people began streaming here in search of 'the scene.' The restaurant tariffs reflect Soho's now-dominant chicness, but there's no need to go hungry, or to pay through the nose. You can shell out $35+ for a steak at Balthazar, but you can also eat for plenty less at Fanelli Café.

In bordering Tribeca, the star element plays a big part, this time in the shape of actor Robert De Niro. Now one of Tribeca's most famous diners, he moved here in 1976, and began investing in restaurants such as Nobu and the Tribeca Grill. He promoted his 'hood as a cool area in which to hang out, and it still is.

East Village and Lower East Side

While once there was little reason to venture into these neighborhoods, and certainly not at night, they now come alive when the sun goes down, and, for many New Yorkers, the best two reasons to visit the Lower East Side and East Village are to drink and to dine.

The once-mean streets of the Lower East Side, an enclave of immigration in previous centuries, are now very much the domain of hipsters. To witness this renaissance, check out the

Street food in Lower Manhattan

restaurants around Ludlow and Clinton streets. Even the once-lowly Bowery is becoming a restaurant mecca. For a taste of the area's heritage, however, visit Katz's Delicatessen or seek out the colorful, inexpensive Indian restaurants along Sixth Street between Second and First avenues, known collectively as 'Curry Row.'

The bagel debate

The fastest way to start an argument among New Yorkers is to ask them where to find the best bagels in town. The rings of bread dough, first boiled then baked, were introduced to New York in the 1880s by East European Jews and have since become a local staple. They come in any number of varieties – sesame, poppy, onion, raisin, among others – and are traditionally eaten with a *schmear* of cream cheese and perhaps a slice of lox (smoked salmon) and red onion. Uptown favorites include Lenny's Bagels (2601 Broadway at 98th Street) and Tal Bagel (333 East 86th Street near Second Avenue). In Midtown, look for Ess-a-Bagel (831 Third Avenue at 50th Street) and Pick a Bagel on Third (297 Third Avenue at 22nd Street). Downtown is Murray's Bagels (500 Sixth Avenue at 12th Street) and longtime favorite Kossar's (367 Grand Street near Essex Street), which specializes in 'bialys,' a close cousin to the bagel but without the hole.

For a look at the East Village scene, check out hip bars and restaurants along avenues A and B, although expect to feel old and unfashionable if you're over 40 and out of sync if you show up before 10 o'clock.

Upper West Side

This part of town, home to the Lincoln Center and the focal point of the New York Jewish community, is good for understated neighborhood dining. Columbus Circle and the Lincoln Center area have fine-dining choices, long topped by Jean-Georges. The arrival of the Time Warner Center

Sweet treats

In Katz's deli

upped the culinary sweepstakes (with price tags) even higher, with Michael Lomonaco's highly regarded Porter House New York, Thomas Keller's 'edible art' at Per Se (expect to pay at least $300...per person!), and the always-booked Masa, current holder of the highest price tag of any Manhattan dining experience. Keller's Bouchon Bakery offers light meals and decadent desserts with a far less stratospheric tab.

Upper East Side

With sky-high real-estate prices and stores to match, the upscale Upper East Side is where ladies of leisure like to lunch. You can dine very well indeed in this part of town, and the neighborhood demographics supply the sort of crowd that appreciates upmarket dining. Many of the neighborhood's best restaurants are old standbys that seem tailor-made for special occasions, or to wine and dine a client or a visiting in-law. The neighborhood has attracted chefs such as Daniel Boulud and David Burke, in search of customers with refined taste buds and big dining budgets.

For the most part, the best restaurants are concentrated in the western part of the neighborhood, on leafy streets lined with palatial townhouses and white-glove apartment houses. In general, the farther east you go, the younger the restaurant crowd becomes – Second Avenue, especially, is noted for its noisy bars and eateries catering to restless single folk on the prowl.

BRUNCH

Weekends are when New Yorkers stroll instead of sprint. On Saturday and Sunday mornings, restaurants are filled with Manhattanites enjoying a slow start to the day, eating brunch in the company of friends, with a partner or spouse, or alone with the newspaper or a book. Sunday brunch in particular is a local tradition.

Most restaurants offer a set-price brunch menu, but there are some stand-out choices. In the heart of Central Park on the edge of a pond dotted with colorful rowboats, the Loeb Boathouse wins the prize for charm. The menu is good, too; try the smoked salmon frittata, French toast or steak and eggs. For the best French-inspired brunch, head for Balthazar in Soho, and dip your croissant into a gigantic cup of the house hot chocolate. For bohemian appeal, head out to Brooklyn, which excels at laidback weekends.

Food and Drink Prices

Throughout this book, price guide for a three-course dinner for one:
$$$$ = over $70
$$$ = $50–70
$$ = $25–50
$ = under $25

A successful shop at Macy's

SHOPPING

There are few more exciting places to shop than this Cornucopia-on-the-Hudson, with its boutiques, department stores, and discount outlets all jostling for a piece of the sales action.

From the 1860s to around 1920, shopping was concentrated in what is now the Ladies Mile Historic District. The heart was roughly from 14th to 24th streets along Sixth Avenue. But as the better residential areas continued moving north in the early 1900s, the stores followed, opening quarters in Midtown, where the larger stores remain today. Shopping, however, is not limited to any one area. Every neighborhood has its share of lures, suited to the tastes and budgets of its residents. A general rule of thumb is that the most elegant boutiques are Uptown, the big department stores are in Midtown, and the funkier boutiques are Downtown. Wherever you roam in New York, shopping is part of the fun.

Opening times vary – the general rule is that Downtown stores open and close an hour or two later than Uptown. Most department stores and many other shops open Mon–Sat 10am–6pm, with evening hours on Thursday. Some stay open until 8pm or 9pm on a regular basis and are also open on Sundays.

Sales are held after the Christmas holidays and in mid-July. Department stores tend to offer the best markdowns. Holiday weekends – Memorial Day, Labor Day, etc. – are also prime sale times. Barney's legendary warehouse sales draw big crowds. For manufacturers' sample sales, check www.topbutton.com.

DEPARTMENT STORES

New York is still known for its department stores, selling everything from dishes to designer fashions. Macy's bills itself as 'the world's largest department store.' Lord & Taylor, a few blocks north, and Bloomingdales at 1003 Third Avenue at 60th Street (entrances also on Lexington Avenue), cater to a slightly more upscale market. A notch higher still are Saks Fifth Avenue and Bergdorf Goodman, both luxury stores selling mostly clothes and accessories. Barney's at 660 Madison Avenue and 61st Street is the *ne plus ultra* for pricey cutting-edge fashions.

WHAT TO BUY

Fashion
Look to 57th Street between 5th and Madison avenues and Madison Avenue above 60th Street for elegant, expensive

Caps at a street market   *In the Strand Book Store*

boutiques, to Soho for high-end fashion, to Fifth Avenue for reliable labels, and to NoLita and the Lower East Side for cutting-edge designs and valuable vintage. The Meatpacking District is home to many high-profile designers. For high fashion at low prices, head for Century 21 Department Store (22 Cortland Street between Church Street and Broadway in Lower Manhattan), where designer labels can be had at substantial discounts. Loehmann's is another discount chain with several locations around town.

Art and antiques

The city has hundreds of art galleries, from major auction houses like Sotheby's to the avant-garde galleries in Chelsea. Traditional galleries tend to be found on East 57th Street and on the upper East Side. Only a few galleries remain in Soho.

A good neighborhood for antiques is 10th and 12th streets between University Place and Broadway. Manhattan Art & Antiques Center (1050 Second Avenue at 56th Street) has dozens of dealers under one roof. ABC Carpet & Home (888 Broadway at 19th Street) has several floors of unique furniture, accessories, and carpets from all over the world.

For flea-market finds, check the weekend offerings at Hell's Kitchen Flea Market (West 39th Street between Ninth and Tenth avenues), Antiques Garage (112 West 25th Street between Sixth and Seventh avenues), and the Green Flea Market (Columbus Avenue between 76th and 77th streets).

Books

Barnes & Noble dominates the market with its multiple superstores. They usually have cafés and weekly readings from authors both famous and soon-to-be. Greenwich Village is a great place to shop for books and records; for secondhand and antiquarian titles pay a visit to the Strand Book Store. (They also stock a seasonal kiosk at the southeast corner of Central Park.) Some unusual specialty shops include Books of Wonder for children (18 West 18th Street between Fifth and Sixth avenues), Mysterious Bookshop for mysteries (58 Warren Street between West Broadway and Church Street), and Kitchen Arts & Letters for chefs (1435 Lexington Avenue between 93rd and 94th streets).

Electronics

One of the best places to buy cameras and photographic equipment is bustling B&H Photo-Video at 420 Ninth Avenue at 34th Street (tel: 212-444-6615). Opening hours vary due to Jewish holidays; call ahead.

Another good bet is J&R Music World at 23 Park Row, across from City Hall. And if you want to indulge in the latest iPod, visit the city's fabulous flagship Apple Store on Fifth Avenue.

Some smaller places don't offer warranties on electronic goods, so check before you buy.

A Jazz at Lincoln Center performance

ENTERTAINMENT

From the bright lights of Broadway to the stage of the Metropolitan Opera, symphony at Carnegie Hall to jazz or ballet at Lincoln Center, New York is America's entertainment capital, with a parade of world-class attractions.

Mention New York and most visitors think Broadway, with good reason. New York has been a theater mecca since the proliferation of lights in the early 1900s caused the street to become known as the 'Great White Way.' Around 12 million patrons attend a Broadway show in an average year.

The city has been equally important in music. The Metropolitan Opera, founded in 1880, is world-renowned, and New York has been a popular music center since the days of Tin Pan Alley in the early 1900s. The heritage continues at Lincoln Center, one of the largest performing arts centers in the world, home to eleven resident organizations including opera, ballet, symphony, chamber music, jazz, theater, and film. New York clubs, always on the cutting edge, have been influential in the development of genres from swing to jazz, rock to rap.

THEATER

Besides the dozens of theaters on and around Broadway, New York has several non-profit repertory companies, performing both new works and revivals; many of these go on to take their shows to Broadway. The city also boasts well over 100 smaller theaters with 100 to 500 seats known as 'off-Broadway,' and countless interesting venues with fewer than 100 seats known as 'off-off Broadway.' Pioneering off-Broadway companies such as Playwrights Horizons have nurtured major new works, including *Driving Miss Daisy* and Sondheim's *Sunday in the Park with George*. See listings for all shows at www.offbroadway.com.

For shows offering ticket discounts, see www.theatermania.com or www.playbill.com.

DANCE

The New York City Ballet, one of America's premier companies, has fall, spring and winter seasons in the David H. Koch Theater at Lincoln Center. Its delightful Christmas season production of *The Nutcracker* is a much-loved tradition. Another major troupe, the American Ballet Theater, visits for a spring season at the Metropolitan Opera House and a fall season at varying venues. New York City Center also hosts important dance groups, both modern and traditional, and the Joyce Theater is a year-round stage

A trendy Hell's Kitchen bar

for modern dance troupes from around the world.

MUSIC

At Lincoln Center, Avery Fisher Hall is the home stage for the New York Philharmonic while Alice Tully Hall features chamber groups. Avery Fisher also hosts the annual summer Mostly Mozart Festival. The Metropolitan Opera season runs from October through May, the more affordable New York City Opera performs late October through November and February through April at venues like New York City Center and BAM Howard Gilman Opera House. The Juilliard School of Music offers many free concerts by its talented faculty and students.

Jazz at Lincoln Center has separate quarters at the Time Warner Center that include Dizzy's Club Coca-Cola. Other well-known jazz clubs include the Blue Note and Village Vanguard. Additionally, Harlem has legendary jazz clubs such as the Lenox Lounge. For rock and other music of the day, the Beacon Theater and the Bowery Ballroom are popular.

MOVIES

Film buffs will find a rich menu in New York, beginning with the Elinor Bunin Munroe Film Center and Walter Reade Theater (www.filmlinc.com), home to the Film Society of Lincoln Center and the New York Film Festival from late September through mid-October. Other theaters showing independent and art films include Lincoln Plaza Cinema, the Landmark Sunshine Cinema, the Angelika, the IFC Center, Film Forum, and the theater of the Museum of Modern Art. The Tribeca Film Festival begun by Robert De Niro takes place in late April–early May.

NIGHTLIFE

The city's myriad bars and clubs offer every ambience from refined to raucous, and something for every age and taste. The late night dance club scene frequented by young New Yorkers tends to be found Downtown, in the Meatpacking District or in Hell's Kitchen, on the far west side in the 40s. Hot clubs are often hidden in unexpected places like warehouses or lofts.

Sports headliners

Sports are always in season in New York, and watching a thrilling game is fun for visitors and residents alike. The city offers major teams in every arena: Yankee and Mets baseball April through September, Knicks and Nets basketball October through April, Giants and Jets football September through early January, Rangers hockey October through April, and Red Bulls soccer March through October. The US Open Tennis Championship in late August is a world-class Grand Slam event. For current schedules, see www.nycgo.com (go to 'what to do,' 'sports').

New York saw mass-scale immigration in the 19th century

HISTORY: KEY DATES

From a small Dutch trading post to the 'crossroads of the world,' the rise of New York has been accompanied by civil war, mass immigration, riots and recession, terrorism, and triumph.

NEW AMSTERDAM

1524	Giovanni da Varrazzano is the first European to step onto the island known to the local Algonquin Indians as Mannahatta.
1624	The Dutch West India Company establishes a settlement (New Amsterdam) on the southern tip of Mannahatta.
1664	War between England and Holland. New Amsterdam surrenders and is renamed New York after Charles II's brother, James, Duke of York.

INDEPENDENCE TO CIVIL WAR

1776	The Revolutionary War begins; the colonies declare independence. British troops occupy New York until 1783.
1789–90	New York is capital of the new United States of America.
1811	The decision is made to lay out the city's streets in a grid pattern.
1830	Irish and German immigrants begin arriving in great numbers.
1835	Part of Manhattan is ravaged by the 'Great Fire.'
1848–9	Political refugees arrive after failure of the German Revolution.
1861–5	American Civil War. The city provides troops and supplies to the Yankee effort. Draft riots engulf the streets in 1863.

LATE 19TH CENTURY

1865	Italians, Jews, and Chinese begin arriving in large numbers.
1883	The Brooklyn Bridge opens.
1886	The Statue of Liberty, a gift from France, is unveiled.
1892	Ellis Island becomes the entry point for immigrants. More than 12 million immigrants pass through before it is closed in 1954.
1898	New York's five boroughs unite under one municipal government.

Disaster struck with the Wall Street crash in 1929

20TH CENTURY

1902	Completion of Flatiron Building, briefly the world's tallest building.
1913	Erection of the world's tallest skyscraper, the Woolworth Building, begins. It is superseded in 1930 by the Chrysler Building.
1917–18	US intervenes in World War I.
1929	Wall Street Crash and start of the Great Depression.
1931	Empire State Building opens, the world's tallest building.
1933–45	Europeans take refuge in New York from Nazi persecution.
1941	US enters World War II.
1946	United Nations begins meeting in New York.
1970	The city's economy declines until c.1976.
1973	The 110-story World Trade Center opens, the world's tallest building at the time.
1975	The city avoids bankruptcy via Federal government loan.
1987	'Black Monday' on Wall Street; shares drop 30 percent in value.
1993	Rudolph Giuliani voted in as mayor and gets 'tough on crime.' A bomb explodes below the World Trade Center.

21ST CENTURY

2000	Crowds flock to revitalized Times Square to see in the millennium.
2001	Terrorists crash two hijacked planes into the Twin Towers of the World Trade Center. The buildings collapse, killing close to 3,000 people. Michael Bloomberg is elected mayor.
2003	Power blackout plunges New York into darkness. FBI survey finds New York to be the safest large city in the US.
2004	Museum of Modern Art reopens in Manhattan after major expansion.
2008	Democratic Senator Barack Obama elected the first black president of the United States. Wall Street experiences the worst financial crisis since the Great Depression.
2009	Michael Bloomberg elected for an unprecedented third term as mayor. New baseball stadiums open for the Yankees and the Mets. High Line Park opens to the public.
2011	Occupy Wall Street protesters descend on lower Manhattan.
2012	Hurricane Sandy causes extensive damage to the waterfront and transportation systems.

BEST ROUTES

In the Empire State Building's lobby

FIFTH AVENUE

Few streets evoke the essence of the city as powerfully as Fifth Avenue, with its iconic Empire State Building, glorious Rockefeller Center, stylish shopping, and elegant St Patrick's Cathedral.

> **DISTANCE:** 1.5 miles (2.5km)
> **TIME:** A half-day
> **START:** Empire State Building
> **END:** Grand Army Plaza
> **POINTS TO NOTE:** Try to get to the Empire State Building as early as possible to avoid long lines. Or come back at dusk for sunset and a spectacular view of Manhattan at night. The Top of the Rock offers an alternative view of the city skyline with shorter lines.

Once the playground of Gotham's wealthiest families, today Fifth Avenue is most people's image of Manhattan. Here are the city's most famous skyscraper, best views, landmark buildings, and signature stores.

EMPIRE STATE BUILDING

Rising like a rocket above 34th Street and Fifth Avenue is the **Empire State Building** ❶ (www.esbnyc.com; observatory daily 8am–2am, last ascent at 1.15am; charge). When it opened in 1931, this Art Deco landmark was the tallest building in the world; today, it ranks behind One World Trade Center and skyscrapers in Taipei, Kuala Lumpur, and Chicago, among others. Still, the view from the 86th-floor Observatory is incomparable: on a clear day you can see as far as 80 miles (128km) away.

This is the place where a forlorn Cary Grant waited for Deborah Kerr in *An Affair to Remember* (1957), where Tom Hanks hooked up with Meg Ryan in *Sleepless in Seattle* (1993), and where Fay Wray had a rendezvous with a tall, dark leading man of a more brutish disposition in *King Kong* (1933).

Ticket options

Lines at the security checkpoint, ticket booth, and elevator can be horrendous, but you can save time by buying tickets online. Although you still have to pass through security and wait for an elevator, you won't need to wait hours to get a ticket. If you have money to burn, you could buy an 'Express Pass Ticket,' entitling the holder to move to the front of

At the Rockefeller Center　　　　　　　　*Surveying the Empire State Building*

all lines. For an additional fee, you can also purchase 102nd-floor **Observatory** tickets, which are sold only at the ticket office on the second floor.

New York Skyride
The **New York Skyride** is a simulated flight around the city narrated by actor Kevin Bacon. Unless you're traveling with children, you may wish to skip this, as a virtual experience of the skyline seems slightly redundant when the real thing is only an elevator away. The only

advantage of a Skyride ticket is that it gives you a shortcut to the Observatory.

NEW YORK PUBLIC LIBRARY

Continue north on legendary Fifth Avenue. Although the magnificent townhouses once owned here by such eminent dynasties as the Astors and Vanderbilts have been replaced by less glamorous discount shops, the old grandeur can still be found at the elegant Beaux Arts **New York Public Library ❷** (www.nypl.org; Mon–Sat 10am–6pm, Tue–Wed until 8pm; free access and daily tours) at 42nd Street, renamed the Stephen A. Schwarzman Building after a large donation from the billionaire investor.

With its Corinthian columns and white Vermont marble, its palatial staircases, and famous sculpted lions standing guard out front, the 1911 building is a landmark of its kind. The building's architects were John Merven Carrère and Thomas Hastings, Paris-trained partners who triumphed in a design competition. The grand stone lions at the entrance were sculpted by Edward Clark Potter and are known as Patience and Fortitude, nicknames bestowed upon them by Depression-era Mayor Fiorello LaGuardia.

Reading Room
Not to be missed is the majestic third-floor Main Reading Room, brilliantly renovated in 1998 at a cost of $15 million.

The New York Public Library's Reading Room

Its vast perimeter is lined with reference works surrounding lamp-lit desks, at which readers digest books summoned with 'call slips' from the library's vast hidden recesses. Free tours are offered daily from Astor Hall at the library's entrance.

Among the books, maps, manuscripts, periodicals, photographs, and varied items numbering in the millions in this building are the first Gutenberg Bible brought to America, Christopher Columbus's 1493 account of his momentous voyage, George Washington's own handwritten *Farewell Address*, and Thomas Jefferson's early draft of the *Declaration of Independence*.

Head two blocks north to West 44th Street for a liquid lunch at the **Algonquin Hotel**, see ②.

ROCKEFELLER CENTER

Continuing up Fifth Avenue, a left turn at West 47th Street leads into the **Diamond District** ❸, where close to $500 million in gems is traded every day, much of it by Hasidic Jews.

At 48th Street, you will find the glorious **Rockefeller Center** ❹ (tours daily every hour; tickets sold at the NBC Experience Store), a complex of 19 commercial buildings that were constructed by the financier John D. Rockefeller, Jr, in the 1930s.

Enter this vast 'city within a city' from Fifth via the **Channel Gardens**, a sloping walkway that leads to the base of the **GE Building** (30 Rockefeller Plaza), a soaring 1934 Art Deco landmark that in some ways presaged the skyscrapers to come.

The Morgan Library & Museum

Billionaire J.P. Morgan (1837–1913), known for his consolidation of railroad and steel empires, was an expert collector with taste and wealth, both well displayed at the Morgan Library & Museum (225 Madison Avenue at 36th Street; www.morganlibrary.org; Tue–Thur 10.30am–5pm, Fri 10.30am–9pm, Sat 10am–6pm, Sun 11am–6pm; charge). Around the turn of the 20th century, Morgan acquired entire collections from the most prominent art dealers in Europe and the United States. He bought Chinese ceramics, medieval tapestries, and Near Eastern antiquities along with Old Master paintings and drawings. He also acquired illuminated books of hours, and handwritten letters by Thomas Jefferson, George Washington, and Napoleon, as well as manuscripts by Charles Dickens, John Keats, John Milton, and others. Equally impressive is the building, an elegant mansion with a fabulous library for Morgan, designed in the early 1900s by architect Charles McKim. The modern extension by Renzo Piano substantially increased the library's exhibition space, and added two excellent lunch options, a café, and a formal dining room. A nearby alternative for lunch is the Moroccan-themed **Barbes**, see ①.

City views from the Top of the Rock

Public art

The GE Building is fronted by a sunken courtyard that becomes the venue of an outdoor restaurant during the summer and an ice-skating rink in winter. A towering Christmas tree stands here in the holiday season.

Lee Lawrie's stone-relief *Genius* looms over the building's entrance, while inside the main lobby are two murals by José María Sert, *American Progress* and *Time*. Mexican muralist Diego Rivera was originally to do the murals, but the Rockefellers fired him for refusing to change a panel that depicted Bolshevik revolutionary and Soviet leader Vladimir Lenin. The unfinished mural was shrouded in canvas during the building's opening ceremony and, six months later, destroyed.

Television tour

Before leaving, take a look in the **NBC Experience Store** (entrance on 49th Street; www.nbcstudiotour.com; tours 8.30am–5.30pm Mon–Thur every 30 mins, Fri–Sun every 15 mins; charge), across from the glassed-in Today Show studio. There are quirky interactive exhibits and a collection of memorabilia from the network's 80-year history. However, the highlight is the 70-minute behind-the-scenes **NBC Studio Tour**.

Top of the Rock

Also available are tickets for the **Top of the Rock** (www.topoftherocknyc.com; daily 8am–midnight, last ascent 11pm; charge), an observation deck on the 70th floor of the GE Building. If you don't have time for the Empire State, this is a good alternative, as the lines tend to be shorter, the observation deck less crowded, and the views include Central Park. The observation deck is also glassed in, rather than protected by railings, so views here are less interrupted. The **Rock Center Café**, see ③, is a good refueling option.

St Patrick's Cathedral

ST PATRICK'S CATHEDRAL

Back on street level, a huge bronze sculpture of *Atlas*, also by Lee Lawrie, stands in front of the **International Building**, between 50th and 51st streets. **St Patrick's Cathedral 5** (daily 6.30am–8.45pm; free), on the other side of Fifth Avenue, towers over the scene. Dedicated in 1879, St Patrick's ornate neo-Gothic facade works as an intriguing counterpoint to the angular lines and smooth surfaces of the surrounding skyscrapers. Take time to admire the cathedral's interior, notably its impressive stained glass.

Just north of the Cathedral on Fifth Avenue is **Fig & Olive 4**, another pleasant spot for lunch.

THE PALEY CENTER FOR MEDIA

For a restful nostalgia stop, detour west half a block on 52nd Street to the **Paley Center for Media 6** (25 East 52nd Street; www.paleycenter.org; Wed–Sun noon–6pm, Thur until 8pm). Named for William Paley, former head of the CBS network, this is a rare treasure trove of 150,000 radio and television programs from their earliest days. In the fourth-floor library, you can sit at a screen and have your choice of hundreds of vintage shows, from *I Love Lucy* to *The Honeymooners*. Helpful staff will show you how to navigate. The downstairs auditorium shows films with themes such as 'Funny Women of TV.'

SHOPPING STOPS

From here Fifth Avenue is mostly devoted to commerce, although several churches do counterbalance the materialism to a degree. **Saks Fifth Avenue**, one of the country's best department stores, is across from Rockefeller Center. The super-rich can be seen gliding between Versace, Cartier, Gucci, and other shops from 51st to 57th streets. Don't forget to pay tribute to one of the most famous scenes in American cinema history and look in the windows at **Tiffany's**, in homage to Audrey Hepburn as Holly Golightly.

53RD TO 56TH STREETS

The ornate facade of **St Thomas Church 7** – built in French Gothic style and completed in 1913 – overlooks Fifth Avenue from 53rd Street. If time allows, stop to admire the sanctuary.

Continue to the end of the next block. On the left is the **Peninsula Hotel 8**, housed in a grand 1905 Renaissance building. On the right, the even grander **St Regis Hotel 9** (see page 105) is an Edwardian wedding cake of a building, adorned with marvelous filigree and murals by Maxfield Parrish.

Across West 55th Street from the Peninsula Hotel is the stately **Fifth Avenue Presbyterian Church 10**, built in Gothic style in 1873.

Rising from the corner of 56th Street is **Trump Tower 11**. Step into the lobby of this 68-story condominium complex

Cabs on Fifth Avenue

The Plaza at night

for a glimpse of tycoon Donald Trump's signature over-the-top style, replete with gleaming brass, polished marble, and a five-story waterfall.

57TH STREET

There's shopping galore around the corner on East 57th Street, home to designers including Louis Vuitton, Chanel, and Prada. More casual are flagship stores for such brands as Levi's and Nike.

Need a break? Wander into the glass-enclosed atrium of the former **IBM Building** ⓬ (590 Madison Avenue), where footsore shoppers can have a rest sur-

rounded by modern sculpture, or enjoy a snack on the mezzanine.

GRAND ARMY PLAZA

Beyond 57th Street, it's a one-block walk past upscale department store **Bergdorf Goodman** (women's fashions are in the main store on the west side of Fifth, men's on the east) to **Grand Army Plaza** ⓭, which serves as a gateway to Central Park and the setting of the city's landmark grande dame hotel, **The Plaza** (see page 105). It is now home to apartment dwellers too, but the classic style remains.

Food and Drink

❶ BARBES

21 East 36th Street (between Fifth and Madison avenues); tel: 212-684-0215; www.barbesrestaurantnyc.com; daily L and D; $$
One of the city's best Moroccan restaurants has an inviting lunch menu that includes sandwiches and burgers as well as tagines.

❷ ALGONQUIN HOTEL

59 West 44th Street (near Sixth Avenue); tel: 212-840-6800; www.algonquinhotel.com; daily B, L, and D; $$$
Whether it's Martinis at the Blue Bar or afternoon tea in the woodpaneled lobby, there's a sense of literary history in the space once occupied by Dorothy Parker and other members of the Round Table.

❸ ROCK CENTER CAFÉ

20 West 50th Street; tel: 212-332-7620; rockcentercafeny.com; Mon–Fri B, L, and D, Sat–Sun L and D; $$
Winter views of the ice-skating rink make this a cheery place to enjoy Italian fare (the crab and risotto cakes are a standout). In summer the rink is converted to garden setting.

❹ FIG & OLIVE

10 East 52nd Street (between Fifth and Madison avenues); tel: 212-319-2002; www.figandolive.com; daily L and D; $–$$$
Interesting Mediterranean menu featuring virgin olive oils, paninis, salads and tarts at lunch. More expensive for dinner, with a tasting menu at the bar.

In busy Times Square

TIMES SQUARE TO HERALD SQUARE

Spend a few hours around Times Square and Broadway, exploring the world's largest store and two unique museums, and purchase discount tickets if you want to end the day with a Broadway show.

> **DISTANCE:** 2 miles (3km)
> **TIME:** A half-day
> **START:** Times Square at corner of 42nd street
> **END:** Herald Square, Sixth Avenue and 34th–35th streets
> **POINTS TO NOTE:** Our suggestion is to do some sightseeing, followed by a Broadway show. On Wednesday and on weekends, you could end a morning tour with lunch and a matinee, otherwise start in the afternoon to finish with an evening show.

TIMES SQUARE

New York's 'Crossroads of the World,' **Times Square ❶**, spanning from 42nd to 46th streets on Broadway, swirls with irrepressible energy from the masses of people and the eye popping neon wattage. Yet today it is safer and more family-friendly than ever before, since much of Broadway is now car-free.

42ND STREET

The biggest transformation is once-seedy 42nd Street, now home to Disney theaters, movie complexes, clubs, and the always-popular **Madame Tussaud's Wax Museum ❷** (www.madametuss auds.com/newyork; Sun–Thur 10am–8pm, Fri–Sat 10am–10pm; charge; order online for 20 percent discount), filled with happy visitors taking snaps with the amazingly lifelike wax figures of celebrities from Brad Pitt to Abraham Lincoln.

Theater district

This area has been the heart of Manhattan's theater district for over a century, with a great heritage to be shared. Walk west half a block on 44th Street for **Shubert Alley ❸** and the 1912 Shubert Theater, headquarters for the once-famous impresario. Hopeful actors used to line up here hoping to be cast in a show. Detour half a block east at 45th Street to see the 1902 **Lyceum Theatre ❹** (149 West 45th Street), the oldest continually operating theater, with

The city never sleeps

an elegant columned Beaux Arts facade and mansard roof.

This is also the heart of media land, so look out on Broadway around 44th Street for the second-story **ABC Studio** 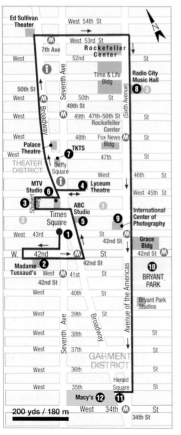 ❺, 1500 Broadway, from which *Good Morning America* is broadcast on weekday mornings, and the **MTV Studio** ❻, where it's not unusual to see squealing teens on the sidewalk, hoping for a glimpse of their American idols.

For available discount tickets, visit the **TKTS** booth ❼ at Duffy Square on 46th Street. The tiered red-glass staircase at the rear is a fine perch for taking in the sea of neon.

For help with tickets for future dates, stop by the **Times Square Information Center** (walk-in only; www.timessquare nyc.org; daily 8am–8pm; free), in the old Embassy Theatre on nearby Seventh Avenue between 46th and 47th streets.

For a pitstop, there are two good options on 44th Street. **Café Un Deux Trois** ❶, a busy brasserie, is between Sixth and Seventh avenues, while **Sardi's** ❷, a longtime theatrical institution, is further west, past Broadway.

You'll see other legendary theaters as you continue up Broadway. The **1912 Palace Theatre**, near 47th Street, was a vaudeville mainstay featuring stars like George Jessel, Bob Hope, and Will Rogers. The 1925 Hammerstein's Theater between 53rd and 54th, renamed the **Ed Sullivan Theater**, presently hosts the David Letterman TV show.

SIXTH AVENUE

The second half of this walk is a change of pace, with enticing architecture, as well as museum and shop-

Radio City Music Hall

ping stops. Turn right at Broadway and 53rd Street and continue to Sixth Avenue and head Downtown. You are walking through a canyon of high-rise glass office buildings, a quintessential New York streetscape. Note that many of the skyscrapers, such as the Time Life Building on 50th Street, have plazas with seating to rest weary feet and watch the busy business world go by. If you are feeling hungry at this point, as well as weary, head to **Au Bon Pain**, see ❾. Located on Rockefeller Plaza, it is a handy place to stop for a sandwich.

On the west corner of 50th Street is **Radio City Music Hall** ❽, the city's grandest theater space. Radio City Music Hall is a landmark Art Deco theater known for its extravagant Christmas shows and high-kicking dancers, the Rockettes. From the massive chandeliers in the lobby to the plush scalloped auditorium, the venue is palatial. Take a tour (www.radiocity.com; daily 11am–3pm; charge) to see for yourself.

Continuing on Sixth Avenue, you'll know the Fox Network headquarters at 48th Street by the illuminated latest news headlines across the building, and will pass the 'Little Brazil' area, so named for its many South American restaurants, at 46th Street. **Via Brasil** (see page 114) is a great place to sample the cuisine.

Photography center

The next stop is the **International Center of Photography** ❾ (1133 Sixth Avenue at 43rd Street; www.icp.org; Tue–Sun 10am–6pm, Fri until 8pm; charge), the world's largest photography museum and school. There are three cycles per year of excellent temporary exhibitions, many including photographs from the permanent collection. This covers the history of the medium but is strongest on leading 20th-century photographers such as Robert Capa, Henri Cartier-Bresson, Margaret Bourke-White, and Diane Arbus.

BRYANT PARK

Bryant Park ❿ is a green garden oasis located behind the Public Library from 42nd Street to 40th Street. Stop here for coffee and a snack.

Bryant Park is the scene of much activity: a carousel, an outdoor reading room stocked with books and magazines, and chess tables. The park also hosts outdoor movies in summer and the city's only free ice skating in winter.

LANDMARK ARCHITECTURE

Across from Bryant Park on 40th Street are two landmark New York buildings worth a short detour. Look up above the ground-floor shops to appreciate **Bryant Park Studios**, 80 West 40th at the corner of Sixth Avenue. It was built in 1901 in Beaux Arts style by an artist who insisted on huge windows to capture natural light.

Sunny Bryant Park

Herald Square

Such notables as the photographer Edward Steichen and the painter Fernand Léger once had studios in the building, which is currently occupied by many design firms.

The former American Standard Building at 40 West 40th Street, an early design by Raymond Hood of Rockefeller Center fame, was built in 1923–4 of dark brick topped with gold, so that when illuminated at night the building resembles a glowing radiator coil. It was recently converted into the **Bryant Park Hotel**, but the elaborate landmark facade could not be altered.

HERALD SQUARE

Now make your way to 35th Street and a chance to relax and regroup in **Herald Square ⑪**, converted into a small green city park with seating under shady umbrellas, a kiosk selling refreshments and that rare amenity, a well-maintained public bathroom. It is the perfect place to relax before heading across the street to the world's largest store.

MACY'S

Founded in 1858 on 14th Street, **Macy's ⑫** moved to this location in 1902, when it installed the first escalators seen in a department store. You can still see some of the original wooden escalators today. Nine shopping floors and a cellar store stretching for a square block will surely hold something to tempt shoppers.

If you prefer a Broadway show to shopping, Times Square is just one stop away, Uptown on the N or R subway train from 34th Street.

Food and Drink

❶ CAFÉ UN DEUX TROIS
123 West 44th Street (between Broadway and Sixth Avenue); tel: 212-354-4148; www.cafeundeuxtrois.com; daily B, L and D; $$
This large, hectic pre-theater favorite is a good choice for reliable, if not spectacular, brasserie fare, notably decent *pommes frites*. Crayons and butcher paper keep fidgety kids occupied.

❷ SARDI'S
234 West 44th Street (between Broadway and Eighth Avenue); tel: 212-221-8440; www.sardis.com; Tue–Sun L and D; $$–$$$
Diners are surrounded by the caricatures of Broadway stars at this theater-district institution. Great for lunch or a pre-show meal.

❸ AU BON PAIN
30 Rockefeller Plaza (50th Street between Fifth and Sixth avenues); tel: 212-757-4628; www.aubonpain.com; daily B, L, and D; $
When all you want is a good, inexpensive sandwich, this chain delivers, with orders all freshly made. You'll spot other locations all over town.

MoMa's gift store

MUSEUM OF MODERN ART

Since its expansion in 2004, the world's premier modern art museum has been better placed than ever to build on its fabulous collection of Picassos, Warhols, and Pollocks, while further developmnts lie on the horizon.

DISTANCE: N/A – the whole tour is spent in the museum
TIME: A half-day
START/END: MoMA
POINTS TO NOTE: The museum is free to enter on Fridays from 4–8 pm. Audio players can be borrowed free of charge from a desk in the lobby.

The **Museum of Modern Art ❶** (MoMA; 11 West 53rd Street, between Fifth and Sixth avenues; daily 10.30am–5.30pm, Fri until 8pm; charge, free Fri 4–8pm) was a daring pioneer when it opened in 1928 and has been hugely influential in the development of modern art.

A dazzling expansion, completed in 2004, almost doubled the size of the Museum of Modern Art and was the first project for architect Yoshio Taniguchi outside his native Japan. His design has provided soaring spaces for oversize sculptures, and natural light from wide windows and a 110ft (33.5m) sky-lit central atrium extending from the second to sixth floors. The stairwells and pathways with picture windows display art as well as providing views of the sculpture garden and of people moving to galleries through corridors across the garden.

THE COLLECTION

At the heart of MoMA's collection are around 3,600 paintings and sculptures dating from the 1880s, a time that heralded the beginnings of the modern sensibility and a move away from conventional figurative representation.

In addition to these, MoMA's holdings include countless drawings and prints, books, important photo and film collections, and a notable range of functional objects that exhibit good design: from chairs to cups and saucers.

Museum layout
Some visitors will want to head directly to the fifth floor, where the sequence of galleries dedicated to the core collection of painting and sculpture begins; it continues on the fourth floor. You will notice that this is not the sort of museum to arrange art into neat cate-

The building is designed to let in lots of light

gories. Instead, the galleries flow into one another with a minimum of signage and interpretation, reflecting the museum's view that there is 'no one history of modern art.' Their entire collection isn't always on display. If you want to know if you will see a particular work during your visit, use the search function at www.moma.com.

MoMA's third floor deals with photography, architecture and design, and drawings. The second floor contains the contemporary galleries, sections devoted to prints and illustrated books, and a café. On the first floor is a more formal restaurant, the museum's store, and the sculpture garden.

FIFTH FLOOR

In Gallery 1, there are many famous Post-Impressionist works. Among them are Paul Cézanne's *Still Life with Apples* (1895–8) and *The Bather* (c.1885), and Vincent van Gogh's *The Starry Night* (1889) and *Portrait of Joseph Roulin* (1889).

The range of styles grouped together as Post-Impressionists is startling. Contrast Georges Seurat's studies in optical effects epitomised in the seascape *Port-en-Bessin, Entrance to the Harbor* (1888) with Paul Gauguin's works showing influences of African and Polynesian culture, such as *The Moon and the Earth* (1893) and *Still Life with Three Puppies* (1888). Meanwhile, Henri Rousseau's mix of fantasy

and naivety is reflected in *The Sleeping Gypsy* (1897) and *The Dream* (1910).

Pablo Picasso, Henri Matisse, and Claude Monet

The next few galleries take the visitor through the transition to Modernism. The central protagonist artistically was Pablo Picasso. If it is on display, compare *Boy Leading a Horse* (1906) with *Les Demoiselles d'Avignon* (1907), which announced the arrival of Cubism. Picasso's great rival, Matisse, is also well represented. In his dreamlike *The Red Studio* (1911), the artist experiments with color and space and depicts his Paris studio as a flat red rectangle with his works on the walls.

Gallery 9 is set aside for Monet's luminous *Water Lilies*, rendered late in life at his garden in Giverny, France.

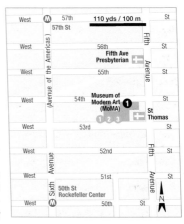

Admiring art

Beyond Realism

Other fifth-floor galleries chart the paths of more great names in nonfigurative early 20th-century art. Here are the Cubist explorations of Georges Braque and Fernand Léger, and the abstract works of Dutch-born Piet Mondrian.

In Gallery 12, the Surrealists make good their escape from physical representation into the psychic world of dreams and the subconscious. Famous Surrealist works include Joan Miró's *The Birth of the World* (1925), Salvador Dalí's *The Persistence of Memory* (1931), with its melting clocks, and René Magritte's *The False Mirror* (1928).

Edward Hopper and Andrew Wyeth

Not that all artists abandoned Realism. Edward Hopper's brooding *House by the Railroad* (1930) was the first painting acquired by the museum. Realism also was similarly embraced by Andrew Wyeth, whose *Christina's World* (1948) is one of MoMA's most popular works.

FOURTH FLOOR

The trail resumes in Gallery 15 on the fourth floor, where works by Adolph Gottlieb, Arshile Gorky and Lee Krasner (who was married to fellow artist Jackson Pollock) embody individual brands of abstraction.

Abstract Expressionism

Spaces devoted to members of the so-called 'New York School' start in galleries 16 and 17 with works by Pollock, whose 'action paintings' were created by dripping paint onto large canvases laid flat on the floor. Equally arresting is Willem de Kooning's *Woman, I* (1950–2).

While these artists were developing a visual language of movement and verve, 'Color Field' painters such as Mark Rothko preferred to work with broad, even expanses of deep color, as in *No. 3/No. 13* (1949).

Robert Rauschenberg and Jasper Johns

Farther along are works by artists who depicted a world brimming with the detritus of consumer culture. Robert Rauschenberg's signature style was objects splattered with paint – such as his *Bed* (1955). Also found here is one of Jasper Johns's 'recontextualized' icons: the potent symbol of the American flag.

Pop Art

Andy Warhol's *Golden Marilyn* (1962) draws visitors into a large gallery (No. 23) devoted to the pop artists of the 1960s and '70s. The theme of Pop Art was consumer culture and the mass media. Warhol's *Campbell's Soup Cans* (1962) and images of celebrities highlight the commodification of images. Often working with silkscreen prints, which he produced serially, Warhol sought not only to make art out of mass-produced items but to mass-produce the art itself. Roy Lichtenstein's comic-book paintings are represented here by *Girl with Ball* (1961).

'War in Vietnam'   *Picasso's 'Woman Dressing Her Hair'*

THIRD FLOOR

The design department on this floor highlights the aesthetics of functional design. There is furniture by designers including Charles Eames, Le Corbusier, and Frank Lloyd Wright, and 'everyday' items such as vacuum cleaners, kettles and computers. Some of the more everyday products on show in the design department on the third floor are still being produced today, and can be purchased in the museum's whizzy, whimsical store on the opposite (south) side of West 53rd Street. The third floor also has sections on photography, architecture, and drawing. The photography department is particularly strong, as MoMA began collecting in the 1930s, well before most other major museums.

SECOND FLOOR

This floor holds the contemporary galleries, displaying the latest advances in painting, sculpture, and installation. Also here are sections devoted to illustrated books and prints. The museum contains numerous excellent examples, representing processes from woodcutting to digital printing.

REFRESHMENT STOPS

When you are in need of refreshment, consider visiting one of the museum cafés, **Terrace 5** ❶ or **Café 2** ❷, or the more formal **The Modern** ❸. After-

wards, you may decide to stroll around the sculpture garden. The garden was designed by Philip Johnson in 1953 and expanded during the 2004 rebuild.

For the foot-weary, consider resting in one of MoMA's three theaters. Movies from a collection of 22,000 (including works by D.W. Griffith, Sergei Eisenstein, Frank Capra, Luis Buñuel, John Ford, and Alfred Hitchcock) are screened most days; enquire about viewing times online.

Food and Drink

❶ TERRACE 5

MoMA, Fifth Floor; Sat–Thur 11am–5pm, Fri until 7.30pm; $

This stylish café overlooking the sculpture garden is a good choice for ice cream, tarts, and a variety of light, savory dishes.

❷ CAFÉ 2

MoMA, Second Floor; Sat–Thur 11am–5pm, Fri until 7.30pm; $

This modern interpretation of the museum cafeteria sits guests at long wooden tables to enjoy panini, antipasti, and pasta.

❸ THE MODERN

MoMA, First Floor; tel: 212-333-1220; www.themodernnyc.com; Mon–Fri L and D, Sat D; the Bar Room Mon–Sat 11.30am–10.30pm, Sun until 9.30pm; $$$$

This dining room serves gourmet contemporary cuisine. In the Bar Room you can enjoy drinks in less formal surroundings.

UNITED NATIONS AND MIDTOWN EAST

A tour of the UN followed by a visit to several Midtown landmarks, including Grand Central Terminal, the Chrysler Building, the Waldorf Astoria Hotel, and the Citigroup Center.

DISTANCE: 2 miles (3km)
TIME: A half- to full day
START: UN Building
END: Sony Building
POINTS TO NOTE: The closest station to the UN is Grand Central/42nd Street, four blocks west. The UN is undergoing renovations from 2013–2015 and certain sections may not be open during your visit. Be sure to check in advance.

This tour covers the central part of Manhattan east of Fifth Avenue, focusing on 42nd Street, Madison Avenue, and Park Avenue, which are home to some of New York's finest architectural landmarks.

UN HEADQUARTERS

Start at the **United Nations (UN) Headquarters ❶** (First Avenue between 42nd and 48th streets; www.un.org; guided tours currently depart from the Visitor's Center, year-round Mon–Fri 9.45am–

4.45pm; charge), which is situated on an 18-acre (7-hectare) campus purchased by tycoon John D. Rockefeller, Jr, and donated in 1946. Technically, this is international territory, with its own firefighters, police force, and postal service.

Architecture

Designed by a committee of architects led by Wallace K. Harrison and inspired by French architect Le Corbusier, the complex is dominated by the sleek glass slab of the Secretariat building. It is, in turn, dwarfed by the neighboring 72-story **Trump World Tower**, owned by Donald Trump.

Guided tours

The only way to see the building is by guided tour, but reservations are only necessary for groups of 20 or more people. Tours start at the Visitors' Center, which is currently at the Dag Hammarskjöld Library Building on First Avenue at 42nd Street, and last around 45 minutes. They usually include a visit to the Security Council Chamber, the Trus-

The United Nations building and New York skyline from the East River

teeship Council, and General Assembly Hall. Occasionally, visitors are also allowed to watch the proceedings of the General Assembly or other committees. (Ask for free tickets at the information desk for this.)

Artworks and artifacts donated by member countries are exhibited across the complex. These include murals by Fernand Léger, a stained-glass window by Marc Chagall, and ancient Indian and Egyptian artifacts.

Japan Society

A short walk a block and a half west from the UN on 47th Street and a worthwhile detour is the **Japan Society** (333 East 47th Street; www.japan-

society.org: Tue–Thur 11am–6pm, Fri 11am–9pm, Sat–Sun 11am–5pm), dedicated to fostering understanding and cultural exchange between Japan and the US. Changing exhibits of Japanese arts are set against a stunning backdrop of indoor gardens, a reflecting pool, and a waterfall. Opened in 1971, the building designed by Junzo Yoshimura was the first in New York by a leading Japanese architect.

EAST 42ND STREET

Head back to the corner of 42nd Street and First Avenue, where a steep stairway festooned with banners leads to **Tudor City ❷**. This classic apartment complex dates from the 1920s, when land along the East River was used for slums and slaughterhouses; hence the windows face west toward the Hudson River.

Ford Foundation Building

At this point you can either climb the stairs or loop around the block, with both options leading to the **Ford Foundation Building ❸**, near the corner of 42nd Street and Second Avenue. Behind its sheer gray walls is a 12-story atrium

Grand Central in the holiday season

Race to the Top

When auto magnate Walter Chrysler learned in 1929 that the proposed Bank of Manhattan on Wall Street would be taller than his own unfinished eponymous skyscraper, he was determined not to be undone in his ambition to construct the world's tallest building and demanded his architect, William Van Alen, add height to the Chrysler Building's spire. Van Alen's rival was his estranged business partner Craig Severance, who, on learning of Van Alen's brief, raised the height of his own tower; he declared the 925ft (282m) Wall Street building to be a world record-breaker in November 1929.

What Severance didn't know was that Van Alen was constructing a 180ft (60m) spire within the Chrysler Building. Shortly after Severance's announcement, workmen hoisted the spire into place, pushing the Chrysler's Building's height to 1,046ft (319m).

However, only a few months later, in April 1930, the Empire State Building was unveiled, with the addition of a mooring mast for airships that meant it surpassed the Chrysler Building by more than 200ft (60m). When the World Trade Center's Twin Towers were destroyed on September 11, 2001, the Empire State again became the city's tallest structure, only to be unseated again by One World Trade Center in 2013.

thick with vegetation; constructed in 1967, the Ford was one of the first US buildings to utilize urban space in this pioneering way.

Superman

Walk west on 42nd Street to the **News Building** ❹ (220 East 42nd Street), an Art Deco skyscraper completed in 1930 and, until the mid-1990s, home to the *Daily News*, for years the nation's largest-circulation daily newspaper. When location scouts were looking for a setting to double as the office of the *Daily Planet*, the fictional paper for which Clark Kent and Lois Lane write in the *Superman* movies, this was the building they chose. Design highlights include the giant revolving globe.

Cambodian lunch

For lunch to-go, sneak south one block and visit **Num Pang** ❶ at 41st and Lexington, where Cambodian cooking is delivered fast and fresh in the form of sandwiches, salads and soups.

CHRYSLER BUILDING

Return to 42nd Street and the **Chrysler Building** ❺ (405 Lexington Avenue). Commissioned by auto czar Walter Chrysler, the skyscraper, considered by many to be the most beautiful in New York – if not the world – and the enduring symbol of the glamorous Art Deco era, features automotive motifs such

Grand Central Station

The station's iconic clock

as gargoyles inspired by radiator caps. For a few months in 1930, it was the tallest building in the world (see box). Inside, the marble lobby, the ceiling mural by Edward Trumbull, and lavishly decorated elevator doors are in stylistic harmony with the Art Deco exterior of the building.

GRAND CENTRAL TERMINAL

Continue on 42nd Street past the Grand Hyatt Hotel to the Beaux Arts-style **Grand Central Terminal ❻**, designed by the architecture firms of Reed & Stern and Warren & Wetmore, which opened in 1913 after 10 years of construction. The Municipal Art Society (www.mas.org) offers guided tours (daily 12.30pm; charge) of Grand Central Terminal. Buy tickets and meet at the information booth on the main concourse.

Main concourse

Enter the terminal and follow signs to the main concourse, a cavernous barrel-vaulted chamber with enormous arched windows. Note the turquoise ceiling, painted with 2,500 stars by French artist Paul Helleu; oddly, the sky was painted back to front. At the concourse's center is the rendezvous point: the information booth, crowned by an iconic clock with four faces made of opal.

At the eastern end of the main concourse is **Grand Central Market**, which shelters numerous gourmet bakers, cheesemongers, and other purveyors of specialty foods.

Lower level and balcony

If you are hungry, there are several options. Head to the vaulted lower level for the **Oyster Bar ❷**, one of the classic New York dining experiences. This is also the place for a coffee break or an informal meal at the lower-level **Grand Central Dining Concourse ❸**. For cocktails in a stylish Italianate setting, try the **Campbell Apartment ❹**.

MADISON AVENUE

When you've done Grand Central, go back to 42nd Street and turn right onto **Madison Avenue**: at this point archetypal New York, with a skyline bristling with gleaming glass towers and streets typically jammed with taxis.

Villard Houses

At Madison and 50th Street, behind St Patrick's Cathedral (see p.30), are the **Villard Houses ❼**, built in 1884 by architects McKim, Mead, and White in the style of an Italian Renaissance palace. The mansions were originally intended for journalist and railway tycoon Henry Villard, who suffered bankruptcy before construction was completed, and were later occupied by the Archdiocese of New York.

In the late 1970s, two of the Villard mansions were incorporated into the **New York Palace Hotel**, where you

Madison Avenue

can now enjoy afternoon tea under a lovely vaulted ceiling created by McKim, Mead, and White.

PARK AVENUE

About a block and a half to the east, at **Park Avenue** between 49th and 50th streets, is another New York landmark, the Art Deco **Waldorf-Astoria Hotel ❽** (301 Park Avenue; see page 106). If you're ready for a break, pull a stool up to the long mahogany bar at the classic Bear and Bull for one of the city's best Martinis.

As you leave the Waldorf, look south down Park Avenue for a view of the floridly ornamented **Helmsley Building**, recognizable by its gold-and-green spire. Looming behind it is the **MetLife Building**, designed partly by Bauhaus founder Walter Gropius. With its absence of detailing and heavy lines, this 1963 behemoth became one of the most despised buildings in the city when it went up, blocking the vistas up and down Park Avenue.

A block north of the Waldorf, between 50th and 51st streets, is **St Bartholomew's Episcopal Church ❾**, a domed Byzantine-style structure built in 1919. The low-level building injects a welcome sense of proportion to the skyscrapers towering around it.

Continue a block north on Park Avenue toward the 1958 **Seagram Building ❿**, designed by Mies Van der Rohe and Philip Johnson and an early exam-

ple of curtain-wall construction (in which the facade of a building does not support any load other than its own). Power lunchers congregate here at the **Four Seasons** (see page 113), one of the city's most distinguished restaurants.

The Citigroup Center

Turn right at 53rd Street and walk another block to the **Citigroup Center ⓫**, at 601 Lexington Avenue. Completed in 1979, the building's angled roof, which was originally designed to hold solar panels, is now a distinctive feature of the Manhattan skyline. The whole aluminum-clad, 59-story structure is propped up on pillars in order to leave room below for the equally modern-looking **St Peter's Lutheran Church**, known for its upbeat 'jazz vespers' service on Sundays at 5pm. The Citigroup's atrium market houses a number of stores and restaurants.

Sony Wonder Technology Lab

As you exit Citigroup Center, pause to look at the distinctive oval **Lipstick Building ⓬** (885 Third Avenue at 54th Street). The lobby is open to the public. If you're craving pub grub in a legendary saloon, pop in for a pint and burger at **PJ Clarke's ❺** on the corner of 55th Street and Third Avenue.

At 55th Street, turn left, and return to Madison Avenue, where at No. 550, the **Sony Building ⓭** (formerly the AT&T Building), designed by Philip Johnson,

rises 37 stories to a so-called 'Chippendale' top, i.e. in the shape of a broken pediment, as in the style of the English cabinetmaker's storage furniture.

If you're traveling with children, consider ending the tour at the **Sony Wonder Technology Lab** (56th Street and Madison Avenue; www.sonywondertechlab.com; Tue–Sat 9:30am–5:30pm; free), which has four floors of interactive exhibits demonstrating the latest developments in digital entertainment.

Food and Drink

1 NUM PANG

140 East 41st Street (between Third and Lexington avenues) tel: 212-867-8889; www.numpangnyc.com; daily L and D; $

Frequently cited as the best place to get a *banh mi*-style sandwich, this tiny shop (beware: no seats) was started by two veteran chefs who combine Cambodian flavors with French baguettes. The pulled pork and glazed pork belly sandwiches stand out, but the soups and salads are also bursting with distinct and fresh ingredients.

2 GRAND CENTRAL OYSTER BAR & RESTAURANT

Grand Central Terminal (42nd Street and Park Avenue); tel: 212-490-6650; www.oysterbarny.com; Mon–Sat L and D; $$

Shellfish rules at this classic Gotham eatery in the vaulted lower level of Grand Central Terminal. Oysters and other bivalves are served on the half-shell, in chowder, in pan roasts, and in 'po'boy' sandwiches.

3 GRAND CENTRAL DINING CONCOURSE

Grand Central Terminal (42nd Street and Park Avenue), Lower level; Mon–Sat B, L, and D, Sun Br, L, and AT; $

For informal meals, a potpourri of stalls offers American and ethnic foods, desserts, and coffee, at reasonable prices. There is ample seating nearby.

4 CAMPBELL APARTMENT

Grand Central Terminal (42nd Street and Park Avenue); tel: 212-953-0409; www.hospitalityholdings.com; Mon–Sat L and D; $$

Jazz Age business magnate John W. Campbell designed this office in the station in the 13th-century Florentine style and used it for work during the day and socializing in the evenings. Restored, it is now an elegant cocktail lounge.

5 PJ CLARKE'S

915 Third Avenue (at 55th Street); tel: 212-317-1616; www.pjclarkes.com; daily L and D; $$

Pouring pints since 1884, one of the city's great saloons operates just as it has for many years, albeit with modern prices. It can be rowdy, but it's a classic.

Central Park's lake

CENTRAL PARK

The heart – some say the lungs – of Manhattan is a manmade recreation area that spans 51 blocks from 59th to 110th streets. The park covers 6 percent of Manhattan. The route below is relaxed, and a good one to do with children. Twenty-one playgrounds provide happy respites.

DISTANCE: 2 miles (3.5km)
TIME: A half-day
START: Grand Army Plaza
END: Central Park West
POINTS TO NOTE: This tour could be linked with a visit to the museum (route 6). Note that it is not advisable to wander the park at night. Check the park's website for details on free guided tours and audio tours.

Central Park (www.centralparknyc.org; daily 6am–1am; free) was laid out by landscape architects Frederick Law Olmsted and Calvert Vaux over almost 20 years, starting in 1858. Creating lush naturalistic parkland from a sparse, rocky landscape was an incredible achievement: almost everything here is manmade.

AROUND THE DAIRY

Enter the park at **Grand Army Plaza ❶** at Fifth Avenue and East 59th Street, where you will be confronted by Augustus Saint-Gaudens's huge gilded equestrian statue of Civil War general William Tecumseh Sherman. A trail to the west leads along the edge of the Pond.

Continue north to the **Wollman Memorial Rink ❷**, used from October through April as an ice-skating rink (Mon–Tue 10am–3pm, Wed–Thur 10am–10pm, Fri–Sat 10am–11pm, Sun 10am–9pm; charge) and the rest of the year as an amusement park. North of here is the **Dairy ❸**, built in 1870 to provide fresh milk and toys to city children. It is now a **visitor information center** (daily 10am–5pm). Check here for tours.

If you're doing the tour with children, take Transverse Road No. 1 west to the vintage **Carousel ❹**, then retrace your steps to the Dairy and follow the path east to the **Central Park Zoo ❺** (www.centralparkzoo.com; Apr–Oct Mon–Fri 10am–5pm, Sat–Sun 10am–5.30pm, Nov–Mar daily 10am–4.30pm; charge), home of polar bears, sea lions, penguins, otters, and over 100 other animal species, and the nearby **Tisch Children's Zoo ❻**.

Strolling in the park   *Winter ice-skating*

Return toward the Dairy, then head north across Transverse Road and Park Drive to **The Mall**, a formal promenade bordered by elm trees and statues of eminent writers.

AROUND THE LAKE

The Mall leads to **Bethesda Terrace** ❼, a two-level plaza overlooking the **Lake**

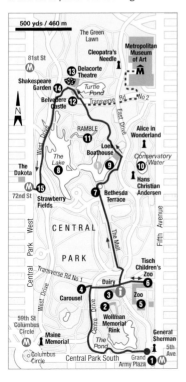

❽ and the architectural centerpiece of the park. On the lake's northeast end is the **Loeb Boathouse** ❾, where you can rent bicycles and rowboats or enjoy a chic meal in the park's main restaurant (see page 115).

From the boathouse, walk east, toward **Conservatory Water** ❿, on which model-boat enthusiasts sail radio-controlled miniature yachts. Note the statues: *Alice in Wonderland* to the north of the pond, and *Hans Christian Andersen* to the west.

THE RAMBLE AND NORTH

From here, explore the trails that lead through the wooded **Ramble** ⓫ toward **Belvedere Castle** ⓬, which is the other side of Transverse Road No. 2. Perched atop a rock at the edge of **Turtle Pond**, this fanciful stone structure, designed in 1865 as a folly, is now a weather station and nature center.

Across Turtle Pond is the **Delacorte Theatre** ⓭, focus of the Public Theater's free 'Shakespeare in the Park' Festival in the summer (www.shakespeare inthepark.org). The **Shakespeare Garden** ⓮ features plants mentioned in the Bard's plays.

To exit the park, walk south along West Drive, stopping level with 72nd Street at **Strawberry Fields** ⓯, a small area dedicated to John Lennon, who was shot and killed outside **The Dakota** apartment building across from Central Park West in 1980.

The Met is home to over 2 million pieces

METROPOLITAN MUSEUM OF ART

The grande dame of New York's museums showcases more than 3 million works of art from across the continents and the ages. The scale is intimidating, so let this museum tour guide you through the highlights.

> **DISTANCE:** N/A – the whole tour is spent within the museum
> **TIME:** A half-day
> **START/END:** The Met
> **POINTS TO NOTE:** Note that the Met is open late on Friday and Saturday. Free gallery talks and guided tours are offered daily. See www.metmuseum.org or stop at the information desk in the Great Hall, where you can also rent an audio guide.

This tour touches on some of the most popular collections of the **Metropolitan Museum of Art ❶** (1000 Fifth Avenue at 82nd Street; www.metmuseum.org; daily 10am–5.30pm, Fri–Sat until 9pm; charge), one of New York's prime attractions, drawing over 5 million visitors each year.

Depending on your starting time, fortify yourself with brunch or lunch at **Sant Ambroeus ❶**, or, if the weather is particularly sunny, go for a picnic in Central Park, directly behind the museum. Alternatively, if you're keen to get started, you could go for a quick bite at the museum's **Cafeteria ❷**, which also offers substantial dishes.

Background

The Met is a palatial gallery with a collection of paintings, sculpture, drawings, furnishings, and items of the decorative arts spanning 10,000 years of human creativity. Featuring works by artists from Bruegel to Botticelli to Van Gogh, it showcases works from nearly every civilization. Exhibits range from flints found in Egypt dating to the Lower Paleothic period (300,000–75,000 BC) up to 21st-century couture by the renowned late fashion designer Alexander McQueen.

The Met's collection was established in 1870 by a group of artists and enthusiasts who wanted an American gallery that would rival those in Europe. One of Central Park's architects, British-born Calvert Vaux, along with Jacob Wrey Mold, designed the museum's first permanent home. The current building has housed the collection since 1880, with its facade remod-

The American Wing

In the Greek and Roman Galleries

eled in 1926. The institution owns over 2 million items, though only around a quarter of the total collection is on display at any one time in its nearly 250 rooms. Additions and gallery renovations are frequent, and the collection on display is always changing. No matter how times you visit, it's always a new place.

FIRST FLOOR

Enter the museum and buy tickets at the aptly named **Great Hall**. The most sensible way to tour the museum is by moving in a counter-clockwise direction, so start with Egyptian art to the right of the Great Hall as you enter.

Ancient Egypt

The Met's holdings in the field of Ancient Egypt are excellent. Statues, figurines, funerary art, and coffins are

arranged chronologically in a series of rooms leading to the Temple of Dendur, a sandstone Nubian temple from 15 BC, dedicated to the goddess Isis, the god Osiris, and the physician Hippocrates. Discovered around 50 miles (80km) south of Aswan, the temple had to be saved from submersion when the Aswan High Dam was built; it was presented to the United States by Egypt in 1965 in recognition of the former's help with saving other important monuments during the dam's construction.

American Wing

Behind the Egyptian rooms is the redone American Wing, which reopened in 2009 after substantial work. The multi-level collection includes furnished period rooms, a stunning loggia designed by Louis Comfort Tiffany for his Laurelton Hall home, balcony displays of ceramics, glass, pewter, art pottery, and silver from Paul Revere to Tiffany. The Charles Engelhard Court wows with 60 examples of large-scale sculpture, mosaics, and stained glass, including works by Daniel Chester French and Augustus St Gaudens.

Galleries of paintings are found on the second floor and showcase such iconic images as Emanuel Leutze's *Washington Crossing the Delaware* and Gilbert Stuart's *George Washington*, as well as works by Edward Hopper, James Abbott McNeill Whistler, and John Singer Sargent.

Peruvian Funerary mask

If you're ready for a break at this point, relax at the first floor **American Wing Café** ③, which boasts views over Central Park, or get even better ones at the slightly more expensive **Petrie Court Café** ④, in the adjacent European Sculpture Court.

European art

Two floors of galleries are devoted to European sculpture, paintings, and decorative arts, plus richly appointed period rooms. The works are hung in roughly chronological fashion, starting with Giotto and his *Epiphany* (c.1320), followed by an unfolding of the Italian Renaissance, with highlights by Raphael, Botticelli, Tintoretto, Titian, and Veronese.

Farther along is Spanish art, showcasing the work of Velázquez, Goya, and El Greco. A section devoted to Dutch paintings includes pieces by Rembrandt and Johannes Vermeer, notably his *Young Woman with a Water Pitcher* (1660). A highlight of the English gallery is Thomas Gainsborough's *Boy with a Cat* (1787).

European paintings and sculpture of the 19th century are grouped together in a separate room on the second floor. Among the many Post-Impressionist works found here are Van Gogh's *Wheat Field with Cypresses*, which he painted while confined to an asylum in 1889, and Paul Gauguin's Edenic view of South Sea life, *La Orana Maria (Hail Mary)*.

Modern art

The Met defines 'modern art' as dating from the year 1900, and ranging over two floors in the back of the museum are exhibits depicting different artistic movements. Although the idea of Modernism was initially controversial (in one episode, a traditional trustee gave reluctant approval for a purchase by covering his eyes and murmuring, 'I just can't look'), the museum nevertheless compiled an impressive collection, including pieces by Picasso, Matisse, O'Keeffe, and de Kooning. Sculpture highlights include the elegant *Bird in Space* by Constantin Brancusi (1923), the ten-foot tall marble *Kouros* by Isamu Noguchi, and the Surrealist-inspired *Eyes* by Louise Bourgeois (1982).

Greek and Roman art

Completing the circular route are the single-level Greek and Roman Galleries, next to the Great Hall. Opened to great fanfare in 2007, the galleries were constructed to house the Met's extensive art c.900 BC to the early 4th century AD. Many of the pieces had not been seen together since 1949, and bring under one roof the very foundations of Western artistic civilization.

SECOND FLOOR

The Arts of the Arab Lands, Turkey, Iran, Central Asia, and Later South Asia

A full set of armor

The Great Hall balconies

opened in 2011 and is one of the more ambitious expansions of the museum, with fifteen galleries highlighting Islamic art, textiles, sculpture, woodworking, earthenware, and arms. Don't forget to tilt your head back in the Koç Family Galleries and take in the majesty of the ornate 16th-century carved wooden ceiling.

The area to the right of the Great Hall's balcony contains a series of rooms showcasing Asia: here you will see a range of exhibits focussing on Korea, China, South and Southeast Asia. Behind them are small rooms featuring Japanese art, plus – for something different – the Met's excellent collection of musical instruments.

In season, from May until late fall, end this route with a well-earned drink at the **Roof Garden Café** ⑤, which has superb views across Central Park. Or visit the museum store, which sells reproduction posters, jewelry, note cards, and an excellent selection of art books associated with the museum's exhibits. It is easy to spend a fair amount of time browsing in here.

Food and Drink

① SANT AMBROEUS

1000 Madison Avenue (between 77th and 78th streets); tel: 212-570-2211; www.santambroeus.com; daily B, L, and D; $$

After visiting the museum, you can charge up your batteries with a shot of espresso, a focaccia or another light bite, and perhaps dessert at this Milanese café.

② THE CAFETERIA

Ground floor, Metropolitan Museum of Art; Fri–Sat L and D, Sun–Thur L; $

A self-service restaurant where hungry masses congregate for a quick bite or full meal from a range of sandwiches, salads, and a selection of hot entrees.

③ AMERICAN WING CAFÉ

First floor, American Wing, Metropolitan Museum of Art; Sun–Thur 11am–4.30pm, Fri–Sat until 8.30pm; $

Enjoy sandwiches, salads, desserts, snacks, or cocktails, with park views.

④ PETRIE COURT CAFÉ

First floor, Metropolitan Museum of Art; Sun-Thur B and L, Fri–Sat also D, AT 2.30–4.30pm; $$

The bistro fare is pricier than The Caféteria, but the room boasts great Central Park views.

⑤ ROOF GARDEN CAFÉ

Fifth floor, Metropolitan Museum of Art; May–late fall Fri–Sat 10am–8.30pm, Sun–Thur 10am–4.30pm; $

Order a glass of wine at the bar and enjoy the views of Central Park and the city skyline.

The Upper East Side borders Central Park

UPPER EAST SIDE MUSEUMS

Some of America's finest cultural treasures are housed in galleries on the stretch of Fifth Avenue between 82nd and 110th streets, dubbed 'Museum Mile.' South of here, still on the wealthy Upper East Side, are two more of the city's notable art galleries: the Whitney and the Frick Collection.

DISTANCE: 2 miles (3km)
TIME: A half- to full day
START: Museum for African Art (or El Museo del Barrio)
END: Frick Collection
POINT TO NOTE: Check museum opening times before deciding on which day to do this route; most are closed at least one day a week, often Monday. A number open late on Fridays.

It would be completely exhausting to see all the museums described in this route in a single day, so the best policy is to choose and concentrate on two or three, according to your taste. Here, we start with the northernmost museum and work southwards through the Upper East Side. Where a museum is noted as undergoing renovations or redevelopment, be sure to check the relevant website before visiting for updates on latest opening times and exhibits. This is particularly true for the first museum on our route.

MUSEUM MILE

Museum for African Art

The long gestating **Museum for African Art ❶** (1280 Fifth Avenue at 110th Street; www.africanart.org; charge) has delayed its opening half a dozen times over the last five years. Let's hope it will be ready for 2014, as was planned at the time of going to press, because it promises to be one of the world's best places to discover the art and culture of Africa and the African diaspora.

El Museo del Barrio

El Museo del Barrio ❷ (1230 Fifth Avenue at 104th Street; www.elmuseo.org; Wed–Sun 11am–6pm; charge) showcases the art and culture of Puerto Rico and Latin America, and was recently renovated with a new facade and café and expanded galleries.

El Museo's permanent collection of over 6,500 objects spanning more than 800 years of Latino art includes pre-Columbian Taíno artifacts, traditional arts, 20th-century drawings, paintings, sculptures, and installations, as well as

In the Neue Galerie

prints, photography, documentary films, and video. Changing exhibits highlight artists both past and present, while special programs offer talks, films, and poetry readings.

Museum of the City of New York

Just one block south is the **Museum of the City of New York** ❸ (1220 Fifth Avenue at 103rd Street; www.mcny. org; daily 10am–6pm; charge), which chronicles the colorful story of New York from Dutch colonial times to the present. The collection encompasses myriad artifacts and artworks related to the city's ever-changing character and phenomenal growth, including his-

toric paintings, vintage dollhouses, and much more.

Jewish Museum

Several blocks further on, the **Jewish Museum** ❹ (1109 Fifth Avenue; www.thejewishmuseum.org; Fri–Tue 11am–5.45pm, Thur 11am–8pm; charge) is located in a fine French Renaissance-style mansion built c.1908. Inside is an excellent collection of Judaica: art, artifacts, photographs, and antiques that tell the story of Jewish persistence in an age-old struggle. The permanent exhibition entitled *Culture and Continuity: The Jewish Journey*; mounted over two floors, illuminates more than 4,000

Museum Mile Festival

A highly popular fixture in the New York cultural calendar since its inception in the 1970s, the Museum Mile Festival (http://museummilefestival.org) is held on the second Tuesday in June from 6 to 9pm and regularly attracts a crowd of more than 50,000 art-lovers and fun-seekers. The whole of the Museum Mile, i.e. Fifth Avenue from the Metropolitan Museum north to El Museo del Barrio, is closed to traffic, and musicians, street performers, and food stalls line the route. All of the museums open for the evening, with special temporary exhibits also mounted to coincide with the festival.

The Cooper-Hewitt National Design Museum store

years of Jewish cultural history. The museum also has interesting changing exhibits.

An excellent option for brunch at this juncture is **Sarabeth's Kitchen** ❶, on Madison, one block east along 92nd Street from the Jewish Museum.

Cooper-Hewitt National Design Museum

Back on Fifth Avenue, the next museum when heading south is the **Cooper-Hewitt National Design Museum** ❺ (2 East 91st Street; www.cooperhewitt. org; Mon–Fri 10am–5pm, Sat 10am–6pm, Sun 11am–6pm; charge), a branch of the Smithsonian Institution housed in steel magnate Andrew Carnegie's 1901 mansion. The museum has excellent collections of decorative and applied arts, as well as industrial design, fulfilling its original mission as a 'visual library' of the history of style.

The museum is in the midst of a renovation that is due to be completed in 2014.

National Academy Museum

About a block and a half farther along is the **National Academy Museum and School of Fine Arts** ❻ (1083 Fifth Avenue at 89th Street; www.national academy.org; Wed–Sun 11am–6pm, hours change seasonally; charge).

This is the country's oldest artist-run organization, founded in 1825 to train artists and show their work. It upholds the custom of members submitting a self-portrait and a representative example of their work: a tradition that fortifies the academy's collection of 2,200 paintings, 240 sculptures, and 5,000 works on paper.

Past members of the academy have included Frederic East Church, Winslow Homer, John Singer Sargent, and Jasper Johns.

The National Academy

The Guggenheim's most famous feature

The Guggenheim

Perhaps the greatest work of art at the **Solomon R. Guggenheim Museum** 7 (1071 Fifth Avenue at 89th Street; www. guggenheim.org; Sat–Wed 10am– 5.45pm, Fri 10am–7.45pm; charge) is architect Frank Lloyd Wright's landmark spiral design, which celebrated its 50th birthday to much acclaim in 2009. At the core of the collection are the works of some of the leading artists since Modernism reared its head in the latter part of the 19th century. Many were associated with movements such as Expressionism, Cubism, and the trend toward abstraction; such painters as Klee, Kandinsky, Mondrian, Modigliani, Léger, Picasso, and Pollock. The museum recently added a gourmet restaurant, the Wright.

Neue Galerie

Three blocks south is the **Neue Galerie** 8 (1048 Fifth Avenue at 86th Street; www.neuegalerie.org; Thur–Mon 11am– 6pm; charge), in a splendid mansion built in 1912–14 by architects Carrère & Hastings, whose New York Public Library reflects the same French Beaux Arts-style influence.

The museum was founded by the son and heir of cosmetics giant Estée Lauder, Ron Lauder, a former US ambassador to Austria with an interest in Germanic art and sufficiently deep pockets to indulge his passion. His collection, much of which was amassed through the Madison Avenue gallery of Serge Sabarsky, focuses on 20th-century German and Austrian art, with works by Gustav Klimt, Egon Schiele, and various Bauhaus representatives. There are also some items of decorative arts.

The museum **café** 2, named after Sabarsky, is an appropriately artful place to stop for a bite.

The Metropolitan Museum

The southernmost point of Museum Mile proper ends with the most renowned of the nine museums, the **Metropolitan Museum of Art** 9 (1000 Fifth Avenue at 82th Street; www.metmuseum.org; Tue–Thur and Sun 9.30am–5.30pm, Fri and Sat 9.30am–9pm; charge). As the museum is so vast – the largest in the United States – we devote an entire route to it (see page 48).

An option for food at this point is **Candle 79**, see 3, accessed by turning left onto East 79th Street.

A pleasant adjunct to a museum visit is a stroll in the **Conservatory Garden** (daily 8am–dusk), a portion of Central Park at Fifth Avenue and 105th Street. Situated behind gates that once adorned one of the Vanderbilt mansions, this little-known oasis encompasses 6 acres (2 hectares) of manicured grounds divided into Italian, English, and French formal gardens. Guided tours are available Saturdays at 11am and Wednesdays at noon in the spring and summer.

A Whitney Museum Biennial exhibit

BEYOND MUSEUM MILE

While in the mood for art, you may wish to visit the Whitney Museum or the Frick Collection; both are within walking distance.

Whitney Museum of American Art

For the **Whitney Museum of American Art** ⑩ (945 Madison Avenue at 75th Street; www.whitney.org; Wed–Sun 11am–6pm, Fri until 9pm; charge), continue down Fifth Avenue and turn left at 75th Street. At the corner of Madison Avenue is a cantilevered structure designed by Marcel Breuer and one of the Upper East Side's bolder architectural statements.

The Whitney was founded in 1931 by railroad heiress and artist Gertrude Vanderbilt Whitney, who, unlike her contemporaries at the Metropolitan Museum, was more interested in live Americans than dead Europeans. Rebuffed by the Metropolitan, she decided to start her own museum and set herself the task of collecting the works of some of the finest American painters of the day, principally Realists such as Thomas Hart Benton, Robert Henri, and Edward Hopper.

Since then the museum has been dedicated to acquiring pieces that represent the full scope of 20th- and 21st-century art. Abstraction is well represented, particularly works by the so-called Abstract Expressionists, or New York School, who rose to dominance after World War II.

The Whitney has long prided itself on a policy of purchasing works within a year of their creation, often prior to wide recognition of the artists; a predilection for being 'ahead of the curve' that has made the museum a leader in video, film, performance art, and other modes of expression not formerly associated with museum exhibitions.

See the uptown location while it lasts. The museum will be moving to the Meatpacking District in 2015.

If you're hungry, try the Whitney's casual restaurant **Untitled** ④, or, for something more elegant, nearby **Café Boulud** ⑤, on East 76th Street.

Frick Collection

Return to Fifth Avenue and wrap up your tour five blocks south at the **Frick Collection** ⑪ (1 East 70th Street; www.frick.org; Tue–Sat 10am–6pm, Sun 11am–5pm; charge), which occupies a mansion built in 1914 by steel magnate Henry Clay Frick. The building itself was constructed around a spectacular collection of art from the Renaissance through to the late 19th century. Intended from the beginning as a legacy to future generations, it remains one of the world's finest testaments to a connoisseur's vision.

The collection focuses on European paintings (including three Vermeers) and furnishings and represents one of the city's most successful combinations of art and environment. The ambience is one of quiet gentility. Leave plenty of time for the central courtyard, a sooth-

Gainsborough portraits at the Frick

ing respite from the city streets.

Each year, the Frick's concert season showcases young classical musicians. Tickets must be booked in advance; see the website for dates of upcoming performances.

Roosevelt Island

For a little bit of outdoor adventure as a break from the museums, try visiting tiny **Roosevelt Island**, which parallels the Upper East Side. It is home to just one church and one supermarket, but it has lovely views of Manhattan's skyline, especially worthwhile catching at sunset. The most enjoyable way to arrive on the island is by the Roosevelt Island Tramway, which you can hop aboard at Second Avenue and 60th Street near Bloomingdale's.

Food and Drink

❶ SARABETH'S KITCHEN

1295 Madison Avenue (at 92nd Street); tel: 212-410-7335; www.sarabeth.com; daily B, L, and D; $$
To-die-for muffins, pastries, and other baked goods as well as fluffy omelets and pancakes make this an ideal breakfast (or lunch) choice for museum patrons.

❷ CAFÉ SABARSKY

1048 Fifth Avenue (at 86th Street); tel: 212-288-0665; www.cafesabarsky.com; Mon and Wed B and L, Thur–Sun B, L and D; $$
In the paneled café on the Neue Galerie's ground floor, visitors can savor the dark coffee and excellent desserts of an old Viennese-style restaurant. Replicas of period banquettes and Bentwood furniture, plus a Josef Hoffmann chandelier, provide a setting that is luxurious and distinctive. A cabaret performance and prix-fixe dinner are presented at the café on selected Friday evenings.

❸ CANDLE 79

154 East 79th Street; tel: 212-537-7179; www.candle79.com; daily L and D, Sun Br; $$$
A stylish setting for sophisticated vegetarian and vegan dishes made from organic ingredients.

❹ UNTITLED

945 Madison Avenue (in the Whitney Museum); tel: 212-570-3670; www.untitled atthewhitney.com; Wed–Sun L, Fri L and D; $$
From restaurateur Danny Meyer comes a sleek take on coffee shop fare and comfort food made from locally sourced ingredients.

❺ CAFÉ BOULUD

20 East 76th Street (near Madison Avenue); tel: 212-772-2600; www.cafeboulud.com; Daily B, L and D; $$
Renowned French-born chef Daniel Boulud combines family and regional specialties with haute cuisine to create classic French dishes.

The Lincoln Center

UPPER WEST SIDE

This route takes you on a tour of the Natural History Museum's dinosaur collection and the Rose Center for Earth and Space, followed by a stroll down Columbus Avenue and a look around Lincoln Center, which offers opera, ballet, and theater, and the Time Warner Center, with shops, dining, and jazz performances.

DISTANCE: 1.25 miles (2km)
TIME: A full day
START: American Museum of Natural History
END: Time Warner Center
POINTS TO NOTE: The American Museum of Natural History is an excellent attraction for children and adults alike. The museum is vast, and we advise that you concentrate on two or three sections, perhaps punctuated with a session at the museum's IMAX Theater. You may wish to end the day with a performance or gig at the Lincoln Center or Time Warner Center.

The apartment buildings west of Central Park include some of the city's most distinctive, like the twin-towered San Remo, and the well-known, turreted Dakota (John Lennon was shot outside here). It's a neighborhood beloved by its residents. Part of this is the fact that the Upper West Side is within walking distance of three of New York's most popular attractions and some of its best food shopping.

You'll need lots of energy for this tour, so be sure to leave time for a good breakfast or brunch before starting. There are numerous restaurants in this part of town; two good options near our first stop are both northwest around 83rd Street: **Café Lalo ❶**, and **Good Enough to Eat ❷**. Alternatively, have an early lunch at the Natural History Museum's **Food Court ❸**.

AMERICAN MUSEUM OF NATURAL HISTORY

If you're traveling with children, one attraction that you shouldn't miss is the **American Museum of Natural History ❶** (Central Park West at 79th Street; www.amnh.org; daily 10am–5.45pm; charge), although there are millions of reasons for adults to visit, too. In fact, some 32 million: the estimated number of artifacts and specimens housed within the museum's 25 buildings, only 2 percent of which are on display at any given time. The museum is so huge that it would be impossible to cover everything

Tyrannosaurus rex

here; instead, we focus on some of the highlights.

Enter the museum via the main entrance on 79th Street; here, a statue of Theodore Roosevelt stands guard. Outside, the steps are a popular regrouping point, where families and school parties study their guidebooks and maps.

Background

Naturalist Dr Albert S. Bickmore had a passion for a natural history museum, and lobbied tirelessly for one to be established. In 1869 he succeeded in helping to found the museum, which began exhibiting its collections in Central Park's Arsenal building two years later. In 1874, US President Ulysses S. Grant laid the cornerstone for the museum's permanent home at 77th Street, although the original building was subsumed by later extensions that included a Romanesque Revival facade on 77th Street and the facade on Central Park West. At the northern end of the grounds is the latest addition, which is dramatically lit at night: a glass cube housing the Rose Center for Earth and Space. This was completed in 2000.

Fourth-floor Orientation Center

If you only have time to see one part of the museum, head straight up to the fourth floor, home to the world's largest exhibition of dinosaur fossils. Start at the **Wallach Orientation Center**, where a film narrated by actress Meryl Streep explains the modern system of 'cladistics,' which organizes living things into an evolutionary family tree made up of

Brown bear diorama

a series of groups with shared anatomical features.

Hall of Vertebrate Origins
Adjacent to the Orientation Center is the Hall of Vertebrate Origins. Here, the evolutionary tale starts about 500 million years ago. Massive armored fish such as the Dunkleosteus, whose head was encased in bony armor, appeared 360 million years ago and ruled the seas. Even more dramatic are such flying reptiles as pterosaurs and real-life sea monsters, including the ichthyosaurs.

Follow the black stripe through a corridor exhibit on the 1994 discovery of an **Oviraptor fossil** in Mongolia. This particular specimen is notable for having died while tending a nest full of eggs, the first evidence of dinosaur brooding behavior; there is also an Oviraptor egg with an intact fossil embryo still inside.

Hall of Saurischian Dinosaurs
Just around the corner, the first of two popular dinosaur halls focuses on the saurischians, or 'lizard-hipped,' dinosaurs. In the center of the hall, representing the two major branches of the saurischian family, are the towering skeletons of **Tyrannosaurus rex** and **Apatosaurus**, both repositioned with tails held aloft for balance instead of dragging on the ground to reflect the contemporary view that they were agile creatures rather than the ponderous, tail-dragging behemoths that were envisioned by early paleontologists.

The Tyrannosaurus is composed of fossils from a T. rex found in Montana in 1902 and 1908. The broken ribs, damaged vertebra, and a facial abscess were possibly sustained in battles with other animals.

Next to T. rex, munching on the tail of a sauropod, is an Allosaurus. Other large theropods (two-legged, meat-eating dinosaurs) are exhibited in displays along the side wall.

At the opposite end of the hall is the world's only display of a fossil Deinonychus, an agile predator about the size of a human. It is shown in mid-leap, ready to rip into its prey with clawed hands and – deadliest of all – the sickle-like claw on the second toe of each foot.

Hall of Ornithiscian Dinosaurs
The next hall covers the ornithiscians, dinosaurs with backward-pointing hipbones. This group includes armored and horned dinosaurs such as Stegosaurus and Triceratops. Also here are duckbill dinosaurs, whose rows of flat teeth were designed for grinding plant matter. The most significant specimen here is the '**Dinosaur Mummy**,' an Edmontosaurus with rare soft tissue, including a patch of skin clearly covered with tubercles similar to those of a lizard.

Early mammals
The next two halls on the fourth floor focus on **Primitive Mammals** and **Advanced Mammals**, emphasizing the

Gemsbock dioramas   *Ostriches on display*

diversity of the lineage. The forebears of the mammalian line were anything but warm and fuzzy, a fact illustrated by the fossilized remains of Dimetrodon, a large lizard-like creature with a spiny sail on its back. More familiar fossils include those of prehistoric marsupials, giant glyptodonts, and an 8ft (2.5m) tall ground sloth.

The last gallery is dominated by creatures that our Ice Age ancestors may have hunted (or been hunted by), including cave bears, saber-toothed cats, enormous rhino-like brontotheres with shovel-shaped prongs on their snouts, and mammoths with curled tusks.

Rose Center for Earth and Space

If time permits, head for another museum highlight: the **Rose Center for Earth and Space**. This state-of-the-art science center houses the **Hayden Planetarium**, an aluminum sphere 87ft (27m) in diameter. The planetarium is split into two theaters: in the upper half is the 429-seat, dome-screened Space Theater featuring the latest space show, *Journey to the Stars*, which launches visitors through space and time to experience the life and death of the stars in our night sky. The lower half houses the Big Bang exhibit, where viewers peer down at a basin-shaped screen onto which laser images trace the beginnings of the universe.

Spiraling down from the sphere is the Heilbrun Cosmic Pathway, a dramatic ramp that ushers guests through 13 billion years of cosmic evolution. The pathway leads to the **Hall of the Universe**, a large exhibition space with displays on star formation, asteroid collisions, black holes, and other celestial phenomena. Near the center of the hall is the **Willamette Meteorite**, an eroded 15-5-ton hunk of nickel-iron forged in a distant star.

A stairway leads from the Hall of the Universe to the **Hall of Planet Earth**, which focuses on the geological forces that reshape the planet. Multimedia displays explore volcanism, plate tectonics, seismology, climatology, and other aspects of earth science.

Other highlights

Fortunately for interested but foot-weary visitors, other highlights are all situated on the first floor. Just to the left of the Theodore Roosevelt Memorial Hall is the beautifully designed **Hall of Biodiversity**, a celebration of the planet's life forms and a call for their protection. The 100ft (30m) long *Spectrum of Life* is an array of more than 1,500 models and specimens, evoking the glorious variety of life on earth. Other displays focus on endangered species and contemporary issues such as global warming, deforestation, and habitat loss.

To the left of Café on One by the 77th Street entrance is the **Hall of Human Origins**, where exhibits tell the story of Homo sapiens, beginning with apelike

Costa Rican stone sculptures

australopithecines to the fully human people of Ice Age Europe. On display are casts of a 3.5 million-year-old Australopithecus afarensis couple walking across the plain and 1.6 million-year-old Turkana Boy (Homo ergaster).

Fans of famous gemstones should head for the **Morgan Memorial Hall of Gems** on the first floor of the museum. Highlights include the dazzling 563-carat Star of India sapphire, donated to the museum in 1900, and the Patricia Emerald, a 632-carat uncut beauty.

Detour for food-lovers

To see the remarkable gigantic food markets of the Upper West Side, detour two blocks west to Broadway. Zabar's, at 80th Street, is a city institution founded in 1934 and packed to the gills with cheeses, meats, coffees, and prepared foods to go. Walk south to 75th Street and Citarella, which boasts the largest seafood selection in the city, artfully displayed like fine jewels, plus gourmet groceries, pastry, and produce. Fairway Market occupies the entire block between 74 and 73rd streets, with produce stands lining the sidewalk outside and floor-to-ceiling displays within of every imaginable kind of food. By now you will no doubt be hungry, and both Zabar's and Fairway are ready to help with their own cafés.

Don't forget to visit the renovated **Theodore Roosevelt Memorial Hall** with its four scenic dioramas; these pay tribute to the American president who was a pioneer in the conservation movement and had long been a supporter of this museum.

IMAX Theater

After such a long tour of what are just the highlights, you may be ready for a rest in the spacious **IMAX Theater**, which is situated directly in the middle of the first floor. Films, usually with natural history themes and occasionally featuring museum staff on fact-finding expeditions, are screened throughout the day.

COLUMBUS AVENUE

Upon leaving the museum, consider a stroll along **Columbus Avenue** ❷, which runs north–south directly behind. The avenue and adjacent neighborhood are home to designer boutiques as well as numerous enticing restaurants and bars, including (from north to south) **Calle Ocho**, **Café Frida**, and **Alice's Tea Cup**, see ❹, ❺, and ❻, so take a break here if your feet are in need of rest. Just before hitting the intersection with Broadway, you'll come across **The American Folk Art Museum** ❸ (2 Lincoln Square at West 66th Street; www.folkartmuseum.org; Tue–Sat noon–7.30pm, Sun noon–6.00pm; charge), an important and

Hayden Planetarium   *An Aztec sun stone*

delightful collection of pieces by self-taught artists from the 18th century through today.

If you're visiting the museum on Sunday, be sure to leave time to browse the weekly **Green Flea Market** on Columbus Avenue between West 76th and 77th streets, where scores of vendors sell crafts, antiques, vintage clothes, and other household items, as well as fresh produce and baked goods.

And if you wonder why there are long lines at the corner of Columbus and 77th Street, they are for the juicy, thick Black Angus beef hamburgers at **Shake Shack** (www.shakeshack.com; daily L and D; $). Begun as a stand in Madison Square Park, the wildly popular chain, which also serves hot dogs, shakes, and custard, now has locations across the northeast and even internationally. It doesn't hurt that the prices are a rare bargain.

LINCOLN CENTER

Once you've eaten enough or spent enough, continue south down Columbus Avenue to 65th Street, where Broadway also swerves to meet you. On your right is the **Lincoln Center for the Performing Arts** ❹ (guided tours every 2hrs daily, tel: 212-875-5350 for reservations; see www.lincoln center.org for performance schedules, ticket information, and links to all the venues), where some 5 million people a year enjoy classical music, bal-

let, theater, and film. It is fresh from a multimillion-dollar renovation that includes a new half-price ticket booth across the street.

In the 1950s, when the city needed a new opera house and a new home for the Philharmonic, situating them within the same complex was a far-sighted idea. So was erecting a sophisticated cultural center in this part of Manhattan, best known for drug-infested 'Needle Park,' and as the location for composer Leonard Bernstein's masterpiece musical, *West Side Story*, which transformed the classic *Romeo and Juliet* story into a tale of gang warfare. Today, of course, this is New York's premier arts center.

The spouting fountain in the middle of the central Josie Robertson Plaza is surrounded by the glass-and-white-marble facades of Lincoln Center's three main structures. The prestigious **Metropolitan Opera** is directly in front, with two large murals by Marc Chagall behind the glass wall.

Music and dance
To the left of the central fountain, the **David H. Koch Theater** is where the New York City Ballet takes the stage. The third side of the plaza is occupied by **Avery Fisher Hall**, home of the New York Philharmonic and the 'Mostly Mozart' summer concert series.

Behind Avery Fisher Hall (next to the Met) is a shady plaza and reflecting pool around which office workers

Jazz at Lincoln Center

gather for lunch. The bronze sculpture in the center of the pool is *Reclining Figure* by Henry Moore; set back from the plaza is the **Lincoln Center Theater**.

Also within the complex are the distinguished **Juilliard School of Music**, the **Walter Reade Theater** for film, and the **Alice Tully Recital Hall**.

Building green

The greening of Manhattan has begun. The city's first fully certified green building is Hearst Tower, just south of Columbus Circle on Eighth Avenue between 57th and 56th streets, the headquarters of the publishing giant whose magazines include *Esquire*, *Cosmopolitan*, and *House Beautiful*. Constructed atop the 1928 Art Deco Hearst building, the 46-story glass tower is designed to minimize waste and save energy. More than 90 percent of the tower's structural steel contains recycled material, as do the carpeting and furniture. A water collection system diverts rainwater to the air conditioners as well as to the three-story waterfall that cools the atrium. Sensors dim the lights when no one is present, and the tower's glass skin lets in sunlight without unwanted heat. Thanks to improved ventilation, air quality inside the building may be better than outside, which, in smoggy Midtown, leaves everyone breathing easier.

COLUMBUS CIRCLE

From Lincoln Center walk south down Broadway to the southwestern corner of Central Park toward **Columbus Circle** ❺.

On the north side of Columbus Circle is the Trump International Hotel and Tower, situated across from the gateway to Central Park. On the south side, look for the **Museum of Arts and Design** (www.madmuseum.org; Tue–Sun 10am–6pm, Thur and Fri until 9pm; charge) in a distinctive building clad with terracotta panels. MAD, as it refers to itself, is dedicated to showing contemporary works in glass, metal, clay, wood, and paper.

Looming above and almost dwarfing Columbus Circle is the **Time Warner Center**, whose asymmetric glass towers look over the stately statue of explorer Christopher Columbus, for which the circle is named. The upscale stores and restaurants here played a key role in the recent regeneration of this area. The studios of TV channel CNN are on the third floor.

If it feels like time to refuel, stop off at **Bouchon Bakery and Cafe** ❼ on the third floor of 10 Columbus Circus.

The Time Warner Center is also the home of **Jazz at Lincoln Center** (www.jazzatlincolncenter.org), with two auditoriums. Visit the **Jazz Hall of Fame**, or perhaps end the day with a gig in the center's **Frederick P. Rose Hall** or cabaret in the Allen Room, accompanied with a dazzling city view through the back wall of glass.

The lobby of the Trump International Hotel and Tower

Food and Drink

1 CAFÉ LALO

201 West 83rd Street (at Amsterdam Avenue); tel: 212-496-6031; cafelalo.com; daily Br; $

A hearty brunch is served daily until 4pm at this appealing café. The bar stays open until late.

2 GOOD ENOUGH TO EAT

483 Amsterdam Avenue (near 83rd Street); tel: 212-496-0163; goodenoughtoeat.com; daily B, L, and D; $

Meat loaf, pork roast, home-baked pies: comfort favorites are prepared to perfection and served in Americana-filled surroundings. The morning rush for muffins and pancakes is worth the wait.

3 MUSEUM FOOD COURT

American Museum of Natural History, lower level; daily 11am–4.45pm; $

The food at the largest restaurant in the complex is several cuts above typical museum fare, with fresh salads, sandwiches, grilled specialties, stone-oven pizzas, and an appealing choice of sweets. The barbecue and ethnic dishes are particularly tasty.

4 CALLE OCHO

45 West 81st Street (in the Excelsior Hotel) tel: 212-873-5025; www.calleochonyc.com; Mon–Fri D, Sat–Sun Br and D; $$

Fans say the mojitos at this sexy Caribbean lounge and restaurant are the city's best. Soft multicolored lights create an alluring, grotto-like atmosphere in the bar, second home to many of the neighborhood's monied young professionals.

5 CAFÉ FRIDA

368 Columbus Avenue (near 77th Street); tel: 212-712-2929; www.cafefrida.com; Mon–Sat L and D, Sun Br and D; $$$

Mexican favorites including enchiladas and fajitas are just the start at this friendly eatery. It also excels with less familiar regional specialties such as braised chicken in black 'mole sauce, tangy lamb, and seafood.

6 ALICE'S TEA CUP

102 West 73rd Street (at Columbus Avenue); tel: 212-799-3006; alicesteacup.com; daily B, L, and D; $

A hundred types of tea and a dash of whimsy make this a lovely place for a light lunch and a heart to heart.

7 BOUCHON BAKERY AND CAFE

10 Columbus Circle (near 60th Street), Third Floor; tel: 212-823-9366; bouchonbakery.com; daily B, L and early D; $

Thomas Keller opened this informal spot to bake the bread for his five-star restaurant, Per Se, and to offer coffees, salads, sandwiches, and quiche, as well as sumptuous desserts.

Two names for Lenox Avenue

HARLEM

America's largest and most famous African–American community continues to enjoy a renaissance, while retaining the heritage, jazz, gospel, and soul food that make a visit special.

> **DISTANCE:** 1.5 miles (2.5km)
> **TIME:** A half-day
> **START:** 135th Street subway
> **END:** Shabazz Market, 116th Street
> **POINTS TO NOTE:** Take the C train to 135th Street and Frederick Douglass Boulevard to start the route. The No. M7 bus runs along Lenox Avenue in both directions.

Harlem's history goes from Dutch settlement to upscale residential area to mecca for African-Americans. Writers like Langston Hughes, musicians, and artists made the area famous in the late 1920s, the era known as the Harlem Renaissance. Decades of lean years followed, but recent arrivals – attracted by the history and property prices – are changing the face of the neighborhood, although the flavor of old remains.

STRIVER'S ROW

From the 135th Street subway stop on Frederick Douglass Boulevard, walk north to 139th Street and turn right for the St Nicholas Historic District, two blocks of townhouses built in 1891, at the height of Harlem's residential boom. Loop up West 139th and down West 138th between Adam Clayton Powell Jr and Frederick Douglass boulevards to see the architecture. Prominent blacks attracted here account for the nickname **Strivers' Row ①**.

On the corner of 138th Street and Adam Clayton Powell Jr Boulevard is the impressive stone **Abyssinian Baptist Church ②**, one of the oldest and most influential congregations in the city. On Sunday mornings at 9am and 11am, all are welcome to join the throng waiting to hear the magnificent choir.

> **①** **SYLVIA'S**
> 328 Malcolm X Boulevard (between 126th and 127th streets); tel: 212-996-0660; www.sylviasrestaurant.com; Mon–Sat B, L, and D, Sun Br and D; $–$$
> Harlem's best-known eatery, always filled with tour groups. Reserve ahead.

Brownstones in Strivers' Row   *The Apollo Theater*

Continue on 138th Street to Lenox Avenue and turn right to 135th Street and the **Schomburg Center for Research Into Black Culture** ❸ (515 Lenox Avenue; www.schomburgcenter. org; Mon and Fri–Sat 10am–6pm, Tue–Thur noon–8pm; free). This is part museum, part cultural center, holding the nation's largest repository of black history and artifacts.

ART AND MUSIC

For soul food while on Lenox Avenue, try **Sylvia's** ❶. Continue on to 125th Street and turn right to the commercial heart of Harlem. Visit the **Studio Museum in Harlem** ❹ (144 West 125th Street; www. studiomuseum.org; Thur–Fri noon–9pm, Sat 10am–6pm, Sun noon–6pm; charge, free on Sun) to see work by contemporary black artists.

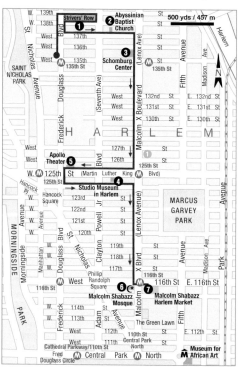

Across the street on the next block is the **Apollo Theater** ❺ (253 West 125th Street; www.apollo theater.org), instrumental in the careers of performers including Ella Fitzgerald and Stevie Wonder.

SHABAZZ MOSQUE

Continue to the hub of Harlem's Islamic community, marked by the green domed roof of the **Malcolm Shabazz Mosque** ❻ on the corner of Lenox Avenue, where Malcolm X once worshipped. Turn east on 116th Street for a unique shopping stop, the **Malcolm Shabazz Harlem Market** ❼. Past the gates of miniature minarets are stalls selling African art, drums, masks, and clothing.

THE CLOISTERS

Far from the hustle of Midtown Manhattan is this repository of medieval culture set in a complex of reconstructed monasteries, and curated by the Metropolitan Museum of Art.

DISTANCE: N/A – the whole tour is spent within The Cloisters
TIME: A half-day
START/END: The Cloisters
POINTS TO NOTE: Take the M4 bus to the last stop (Fort Tryon Park–The Cloisters). Or, if you don't mind a short walk, take the A train to 190th Street, exit by elevator, and walk north on Margaret Corbin Drive for 10 minutes.

If the city's frenetic pace is getting on your nerves, consider a serene journey to **The Cloisters** ❶ (Fort Tryon Park; www. metmuseum.org; Mar–Oct daily 10am–5.15pm, Nov–Feb daily 10am–4.45pm; guided tours daily at 3pm; charge). Perched on a rocky bluff overlooking the Hudson River at Manhattan's northern tip, this branch of the Met is dedicated to medieval art and architecture. Much of the building is reconstructed from pieces of 12th-century monasteries.

The financial force behind the institution, as with so many others in New York, was John D. Rockefeller, Jr. But the man who was responsible for the treasures on display here was George Grey Barnard, a sculptor and collector who scoured the French countryside for church sculpture and architectural fragments. The result is that The Cloisters is an enchanting composite that evokes the hushed atmosphere of an ecclesiastical retreat. It's tranquil, fascinating, and as far away from the city as you can get without leaving Manhattan.

UPPER LEVEL

The Cloisters is on two levels. On the **upper level**, the *Unicorn Tapestries*, woven in Brussels in about 1500, have long been seen as the crown jewels of the museum's collection. The images depict the hunt of the mythological unicorn, whose capture, death, and restoration may represent the incarnation, death, and resurrection of Jesus Christ.

Three of the five cloisters are also on this floor. Directly in front of the room containing the *Unicorn Tapestries* is the **Cuxa Cloister**, from a Benedictine monastery in southern France. The Roman-

The garden at the Cloisters

esque marble capitals on the columns are characterized by intricately carved scrolling leaves, acanthus blossoms, and animals with two bodies and a common head. A fountain in the center of the enclosed garden divides the space into four grassy quadrants, each with a fruit tree and bordered by herbs and flowers.

Romanesque Hall

Separating two of the cloisters is the **Romanesque Hall**. Visitors enter through a massive rounded arch. Crafted around 1150, the arch's capitals are carved in low relief with floral and animal motifs. Across from this entrance is a mid-13th-century, pointed Gothic archway. A third doorway, the late 12th-century Reugny Door from the Loire Valley, has a pointed, recessed arch.

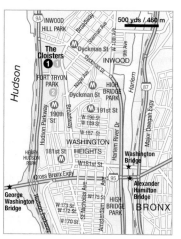

There are two chapels off the hall. Under the altar canopy in **Langon Chapel** is a wooden sculpture of the Virgin and Child. The **Fuentidueña Chapel**, with its imposing rounded apse, was originally a part of the church of San Martín in the Spanish village of Fuentidueña, north of Madrid.

Parallel to the Fuentidueña Chapel is the French **Saint-Guilhem, Cloister**, which is from the Benedictine abbey of St-Guilhem-le-Désert, founded in 804 in southern France.

Pontaut Chapter House

Leading off the Cuxa Cloister are several impressive rooms. Just to the left is a reconstruction of the **Pontaut Chapter House** from Notre-Dame-de-Pontaut, a 12th-century abbey in southwestern France.

Walking in a counterclockwise direction leads to the **Early Gothic Hall,** where the stained-glass windows are superb examples of the new style that was succeeding the Romanesque in churches throughout Europe in the 12th century. Statuary displayed here includes the sandstone *Virgin* (c.1250) from the cathedral in Strasbourg, and the limestone *Virgin and Child* from the Ile-de-France of the mid-14th century.

In the next room are fragments of the Nine Heroes Tapestries, part of a 15th-century series of French pictorial textiles. The subjects of the tapestries are heroes from pagan, Hebrew, and Christian history and mythology.

Stained glass depicting a scene from the Ephesus legend

Boppard and Campin Rooms

The **Boppard Room** contains ornate canopies with intricate twisting arches that frame six late Gothic stained-glass panels originally installed in a church at Boppard am Rhine. Adjacent, in the **Campin Room**, secular and religious themes are blended by 15th-century painter Robert Campin in his three-paneled Altarpiece of the Annunciation.

The Merode Room leads to the **Late Gothic Hall**. Sculptures dating from the latter part of the 15th century represent the Magi who visited Jesus after his birth. Parallel to the Late Gothic Hall is the third cloister, the **Froville Arcade**, built around nine pointed arches from a Benedictine priory.

LOWER LEVEL

Stairs from the upper level lead down to the **Glass Gallery**, where stained glass, sculpture, and tapestries are representative of late medieval works created for the burgeoning class of wealthy merchants and tradesmen, as well as for churches.

In the Glass Gallery are doorways leading to the other two cloisters. The **Trie-en-Bigorre Cloister** displays ornate carved capitals from the Carmelite convent and other religious orders in the Bigorre region of south-western France, as well as from monasteries near Toulouse. If you're feeling hungry at this point, the **Trie Café** ❶ is open from April to October.

Next door, the larger, late 13th- or early 14th-century **Bonnefont Cloister** has capitals and columns extracted from the Cistercian abbey at Bonnefont-en-Comminges. The simplicity of the capitals here is indicative of the strict asceticism of the monks, who considered ornamentation a distraction from the contemplation of God.

Gothic Chapel

The final room is the **Gothic Chapel**, where the effigy of crusader knight Jean d'Alluye lies upon his tomb. There are several stained-glass windows in this chapel, as well as funerary monuments, including the tombs of the Spanish counts of Urgell.

When you've finished exploring The Cloisters, stroll through Fort Tryon Park to have a bite at the **New Leaf Restaurant & Bar** ❷.

Food and Drink

❶ TRIE CAFÉ

The Cloisters; April–Oct Tue–Sun L; $

Visitors can enjoy sweets and sandwiches at a café in the walkway of a French cloister.

❷ NEW LEAF RESTAURANT & BAR

Fort Tryon Park; tel: 212-568-5323; Tue–Fri L and D, Sat Br, Sun Br and D; $$

At the southern entrance to Fort Tryon Park is this airy, oak-paneled café in a restored 1930s building, which turns out creative salads, sandwiches, and beef and chicken dishes. Live jazz on some Friday nights.

The Flatiron area from above

FLATIRON, SOFI, UNION SQUARE, AND CHELSEA

This route takes in some of Downtown's most innovative neighborhoods and sights: New York's first skyscraper, the Flatiron Building, buzzy Union Square, and artistic Chelsea.

DISTANCE: 2.5 miles (4km)
TIME: A half-day
START: Flatiron Building
END: Hotel Chelsea
POINTS TO NOTE: The best days for this tour are Monday, Wednesday, Friday, or Saturday, when farmers come to Union Square for the Greenmarket. Note that most of Chelsea's galleries close on Monday.

Start this low-key, low-rise route at the corner of 23rd Street and Fifth Avenue. Fuel up on espresso or fortify yourself with some imported delicacies from the massive Italian food market **Eataly** ❶. Then continue on to the east side of Broadway at 23rd Street by the Fuller Building, which is better known as the **Flatiron Building** ❶ because of its distinctive triangular shape.

Designed by renowned Chicago architect Daniel Burnham for the awkwardly shaped plot of land dividing Broadway and Fifth Avenue at 23rd, and constructed in 1902, the 285ft (87m) edifice was the first of the city's steel-frame skyscrapers and for a short time it enjoyed the status of being the tallest building in the world.

Rising 22 stories, the Flatiron was immortalized in 1903 in a classic black-and-white shot by the American Modernist photographer Alfred Stieglitz, who described it as looking 'like a monster steamer.'

SOFI

This neighborhood is commonly known as the Flatiron District, home to publishers and a myriad small offices. Head south along Broadway – it's a 10-minute walk to Union Square – making your way along a stretch that was once known as the 'Ladies Mile'. In the latter part of the 19th century, this district ranged along Broadway and Sixth Avenue, from 23rd Street down to 9th Street. It is named for the number of fine department stores that operated here at that time; today, modern chains continue the fashion business.

Union Square Farmers' Market

Theodore Roosevelt Birthplace

On the walk to Union Square, you can make a left turn onto East 20th Street, and dip into the Gramercy neighborhood to visit the **Theodore Roosevelt Birthplace ❷** (No. 28; www.nps.gov/thrb; Tue–Sat 9am–5pm, tours hourly 10am–4pm; free), a 1920s replica of the brownstone where the 26th US president was born in 1858 and spent his boyhood. After his death in 1919 it was rebuilt and rooms were recreated to show how a wealthy family such as the Roosevelts would have lived in the mid-19th century.

UNION SQUARE

A little farther south is **Union Square ❸**, named for its location at the busy convergence of Broadway and Fourth Avenue. This was a stylish area in the mid-1850s but was abandoned by the genteel set by the turn of the century. The square was notorious in the years before World War I as a platform for political demonstrations. Rallies drew crowds through the 1930s, but the lure of radicalism dwindled, and the area went into a long decline.

However, today's Union Square brims with life, a resurgence attributable in no small degree to the **Greenmarket** (Mon, Wed, Fri, Sat 8am–6pm), the biggest and best of the city's farmers' markets, held four days a week at the square's northern end (see box).

Adding to the regeneration has been the influx of publishers, advertising agencies, and other fashionable media firms into the area. The Union Square Partnership supplies the park with free WiFi, and Manhattanites can be seen tapping on laptops and mobile devices as they relax on the park's crowded benches.

In Chelsea Market

CHELSEA

To the west of Union Square (from 14th up to about 20th Street) is fun, sophisticated, and arty Chelsea, a favorite neighborhood of New York's gay population. It is a mix of commercial streets and leafy residential areas. Eighth Avenue is a hub for dining, especially near the Joyce Theater (175 Eighth Avenue; www.joyce.org), an important showcase for modern dance troupes. Walk west to Ninth Avenue and you'll come to **Chelsea Market** ❹ (75 Ninth Avenue, 15th to 16th streets; www.chelseamarket.com; Mon–Sat 7am–9pm, Sun 8am–8pm). An ambitious renovation transformed what were 18 buildings erected between 1883 and 1930 as a Nabisco bakery turning out Saltines and Oreos into a fantastic indoor food market. Much of the original brickwork and steel remain. The interior has a waterfall and sculptured seating, around which are gourmet shops, stores, and informal restaurants, such as **Hale and Hearty Soups** ❷.

Chelsea Historic District
After looking around the market, walk north on Ninth Avenue into the **Chelsea Historic District**, which stretches between Eighth and Tenth avenues from 19th to 23rd streets. The land was inherited in 1813 by Clement Clarke Moore, then sold, with restrictions on development that have helped to preserve its elegant architecture. Moore is

famed for writing *A Visit from St Nicholas*, which became the modern-day *'Twas the Night Before Christmas*.

On 21st Street between Ninth and Tenth avenues look for the main entrance to the 19th-century **General Theological Seminary** ❺ (175 Ninth Avenue; www.gts.edu; Mon–Fri

---

The Greenmarket

If you were to ask celebrity chefs with restaurants near Union Square Park where they buy their ingredients, many could simply point out the window to the patches of concrete and the farmstands that are set up every Monday, Wednesday, Friday, and Saturday. The Union Square Greenmarket is more than a place to find apples in the fall and peaches in the summer. It is a community meeting place and essential source of produce for many New Yorkers, including those who make a living out of making meals.

Organic, and often exotic, meats are available alongside hand-tied pretzels and goat's cheese. In peak seasons, as many as 140 vendors will be offering their products, and the variety is astounding. In summer, you can easily find supplies for a gourmet picnic, including wine, artisan bread and homemade jams. And those celebrity chefs who shop there, also do cooking demonstrations there. For more information visit www.grownyc.org.

The IAC Building

9am–5pm; free), the first seminary of the Episcopal Church. Register at the information desk, pick up a free walking tour pamphlet, and pass into an attractive tree-lined quadrangle that shelters buildings including the Chapel of the Good Shepherd and St Mark's Library.

Gallery district

When you've completed your tour of the seminary, continue up Ninth Avenue, turn left at 22nd Street, and cross under the High Line for the heart of the area's gallery district. When priced out of Soho in the 1980s and 1990s, many art dealers began moving to this former industrial neighborhood, between Tenth and Eleventh avenues. Today there are some 300 galleries. The **Chelsea Art Museum** ❻ (www.chelseaartmuseum. org; Tue–Sat 11am–6pm, Thur until 8pm; charge), housed in an 1850 warehouse building, artfully showcases the work of interesting contemporary artists. The gallery throngs have brought good restaurants to the area, such as **The Red Cat** ❸.

Chelsea Piers

If you prefer sport to art, stop by **Chelsea Piers** ❼, west across Eleventh Avenue. Until 1930 this waterfront served the Cunard and Star lines. After decades of neglect it has been reborn as a sports-and-entertainment complex stretching from 23rd to 17th streets, with roller rinks, ice rinks, a driving range, bowling alleys, batting cages, and a climbing wall. Dinner, wine-tasting and music cruises are available at the marina, and beers and pub fare are served at the **Chelsea Brewing Company** ❹. With fine views across the river, this is a perfect place for sunsets.

IAC Building

Across Eleventh Avenue at 18th Street you can't miss the glass-clad **IAC Building** ❽. Designed by architect Frank Gehry and completed in 2007, the curvy, sail-like form was inspired by Gehry's love of boats.

Gallery-hopping

The boundaries of the Chelsea Gallery District have expanded enormously since this former industrial area first shook off its dusty image in the 1980s. It now extends roughly from 18th to 27th streets, mostly between Tenth and Eleventh avenues. Galleries are in quarters on the street or stacked up in vertical malls, where the elevator opens to a different gallery on each floor. The website http://www.oneartworld.com contains lists of shows and receptions. The most sociable time of year is between September and December, when it's not uncommon for the area to play host to up to six receptions on the same night. Most galleries are closed Sun–Mon.

Outside the iconic Hotel Chelsea

Chelsea Hotel

Head up Eleventh Avenue and turn right onto 23rd Street. Between Eighth and Seventh avenues is **Hotel Chelsea** ❾ (222 West 23rd Street), a landmark of bohemian decadence and the second home of Beat poets, Warhol drag queens, and strung-out rock stars.

This is where poet Dylan Thomas was staying when he died in 1953; where Andy Warhol filmed *Chelsea Girls* in 1967; and where punk rocker Sid Vicious allegedly murdered his girlfriend Nancy Spungen in 1978 before dying of a drugs overdose.

The hotel has been under renovation for years and if/when it reopens, it certainly won't retain that grungy grandeur of old, but for a time-traveling experience, grab a drink or a meal next door at **El Quijote** ❺.

Food and Drink

❶ EATALY

200 Fifth Avenue (at 23rd Street); tel: 212-229-2560; www.eataly.com; daily L and D; $-$$$

From Mario Batali and the Bastianich family comes a multi-storied marketplace and food court with cheese, pizza, beer, panini, pasta, espresso, gelato, and every other Italian delicacy you can imagine.

❷ HALE AND HEARTY SOUPS

Chelsea Market, 75 Ninth Avenue; tel: 212-255-2400; www.haleandhearty.com; daily B, L, and D; $

Nothing hits the spot on a cold day like a steaming bowl of thick, flavorful soup and a slab of sourdough or seven-grain bread at this busy spot.

❸ THE RED CAT

227 Tenth Avenue (between 23rd and 24th streets); tel: 212-242-1122; www.theredcat. com; daily D, Tue–Sat L; $$

Gallery-hoppers gather at this welcoming, art-filled café in the heart of Chelsea's gallery district. The innovative New American chef does good things with classics like roast chicken or Atlantic salmon.

❹ CHELSEA BREWING COMPANY

Chelsea Piers, West Side Highway at 20th Street (Pier 59); tel: 212-336-6440; www. chelseabrewingco.com; daily L and D; $–$$

Choose from 20 handcrafted beers at this microbrewery on Pier 59. You can hang out at one of the long mahogany bars, or on the terrace, or enjoy a full meal in a restaurant overlooking the Hudson River.

❺ EL QUIJOTE

226 West 23rd Street (between Seventh and Eighth avenues); tel: 212-929-1855; www. elquijoterestaurant.com; daily L and D; $$–$$$

A traditional Spanish mainstay next to Hotel Chelsea, with a great bargain: the lobster dinner.

Washington Square Park hosts many events

GREENWICH VILLAGE

Take in notable sights, shops, bars, and cafés on this route around what was once North America's foremost bohemian neighborhood, plus a foray into the trendy precincts of the Meatpacking District.

DISTANCE: 2.5 miles (4km)
TIME: A half- to full day
START: Intersection of Bleecker and MacDougal streets
END: West 14th Street and Tenth Avenue
POINTS TO NOTE: West 4th Street/ Washington Square is the closest subway station to the starting point. Head south a few blocks along Sixth Avenue to reach Bleecker Street.

Start this walking tour near the intersection of Bleecker and MacDougal streets. **Caffe Reggio** ❶, is one of the last of the classic cafés where you can sip coffee at a sidewalk table and recall bygone days, when artists, anarchists, and advocates of free love ranging from Edna St Vincent Millay and e. e. cummings to Jackson Pollock, Jack Kerouac, and Bob Dylan made 'the Village' the epicenter of New York's bohemian culture. Alternatively, head west up Bleecker and turn right onto Cordelia Street for cosy **Home** ❷.

WASHINGTON SQUARE

Walk three blocks up MacDougal Street to **Washington Square Park** ❶. Originally a potter's field and gathering place for public hangings, the park later became the residential center of the well-to-do New Yorkers portrayed in Henry James's classic novel *Washington Square*.

A colorful history is buried beneath the layers of concrete – at one time it served as a graveyard for the indigent and unknown. In 1888, Mark Twain took a train from Connecticut to meet Robert Louis Stevenson and they sat on the park benches discussing the writerly life, a moment immortalized by artist Francis Luis Mora. On the same benches is where, according to his autobiography, Marlon Brando first got drunk and passed out. A group of concerned citizens including Eleanor Roosevelt, who lived on Washington Square West, successfully campaigned to have car traffic removed from the park.

Nowadays the park serves variously as a town square, performance space,

| Greenwich apartments | Life imitating art in the West Village |

and unofficial campus for New York University, which owns most of the large modern buildings around the edges. Its everyday mix of students, chess hustlers, tourists, and carriage-pushing moms is a showcase of the social contrasts that animate the neighborhood.

On the north side of the park, serving as a gateway to Fifth Avenue, is the **Washington Arch ❷**, built in wood in 1892 to commemorate the centennial of George Washington's presidential inauguration and later replaced by this marble version. **North Square ❸**, at the corner of Waverly Place, in the Washington Square Hotel, is a good choice for lunch.

Thankfully, nyu has spared the fine townhouses on Washington Square North, which are about the only 19th-century buildings still facing the park, apart from **Judson Memorial Church** on the opposite side. The church was designed in Romanesque Revival style by architect Stanford White in the early 1890s and is associated these days with a broad range of progressive issues and events, including a series of theatrical performances, gay lectures, and art exhibits.

Washington Mews

Walk about half a block up Fifth Avenue to **Washington Mews ❸** (gates closed

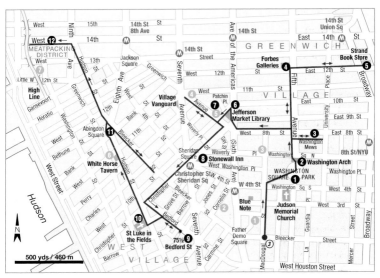

In Jefferson Market Library

at night), a cobbled alley that runs between Fifth and University Place. The pretty little row houses here were originally built as stables for the townhouses on Washington Square North and were later converted to artist studios.

If the idea of an eclectic collection of historical curiosities interests you, make a detour a few blocks north along Fifth Avenue to the **Forbes Galleries** ❹ (see box). Book-lovers should visit the **Strand Book Store** ❺ (three blocks east on 12th Street and Broadway; www.strandbooks. com; Mon–Sat 9.30am–10.30pm, Sun 11am–10.30pm; rare book room closes at 6.15pm), a New York institution. Italian author Umberto Eco describes this as his 'favorite place in America.' The owners claim to stock over two million volumes – from half-price review copies to $100,000 rarities. In 2007, the Strand celebrated its 80th birthday.

The nearby **Salmagundi Club**, at 47 Fifth Avenue, is the country's oldest artists' club, founded in 1870. Its facilities are for members only, but there are walk-in classes (www.salmagundi.org) should you fancy joining the artistic fraternity for a few hours.

Additionally, the Village is home to some of the world's most famous jazz clubs. First among equals is the **Blue Note** (131 West 3rd Street), which presents time-honored greats as well as contemporary acts. Also in the neighborhood, the **Village Vanguard** (178 Seventh Avenue South) cut its teeth by launching jazz royalty like Miles Davis and John Coltrane.

WEST VILLAGE

Back on Fifth Avenue, head west on 8th Street, then north on Sixth Avenue for about a block to the **Jefferson Market Library** ❻, a Gothic confection. Built as a courthouse in 1877 and later attached to a women's prison, this Victorian landmark is now a branch of the New York Public Library. Inmates included activist Angela Davis, Catholic reformer Doro-

The Forbes Galleries

Malcolm Forbes, the flamboyant late publisher of *Forbes Magazine*, who had the wherewithal to indulge his passions in style, shared his tastes with the public at the very handsome Forbes Galleries (62 Fifth Avenue; www.forbesgalleries. com; Tue–Wed, Fri–Sat, 10am–4pm; free). A series of rooms here – the Carrere, Hastings and Picture galleries and a Lobby Gallery – feature excellent changing exhibits of art, illustration and photography, often from private collections of members of the Forbes family. The Jewelry Gallery is one of the highlights, with rotating exhibits such as 'The Vintage Woman: A Century of Costume Jewelry in America, 1910–2010'. Thanks to the generous Mr. Forbes, the galleries offer some of the best free exhibits in New York.

Strand Book Store   *MacDougal Street*

thy Day, and accused spy Ethel Rosenberg. The prison was demolished in the 1970s, and a community garden stands in its place.

Loop around the library to West 10th Street, to find tiny **Patchin Place** ❼, whose residents included playwright Eugene O'Neill, journalist John Reed, and poet e. e. cummings.

Greenwich Avenue

If time permits, take a detour up **Greenwich Avenue**, which has numerous shops and restaurants. If you're in the mood for a bite, **Elephant & Castle** ❹, is found at No. 68, and **Rosemary's** ❺ at the corner of West 10th Street.

Christopher Street

Double back on Greenwich Avenue and turn right at **Christopher Street**. This is the traditional center of New York's gay community. Although much of the scene has now shifted north of 14th Street, it's still worth having a stroll around. Between Waverly Place and Seventh Avenue is the **Stonewall Inn** ❽ (53 Christopher Street), site of a 1969 riot touched off by gay patrons fed up with being rousted by the police. The event is widely seen as the opening salvo in the gay rights movement. (The original bar was actually next door.)

Just across the street, tiny fenced-in **Christopher Park** has a statue of Civil War general Philip Sheridan. Sheridan Square itself isn't a square at all, it's actually at the triangular junction where Grove, Christopher, and West 4th streets meet.

Bedford Street

Follow Christopher across Seventh Avenue South, then turn left at Bedford Street into one of the quiet residential areas that make the Village such a pleasant place to live. The poet Edna St Vincent Millay lived at **75 ½ Bedford Street** ❾, said to be Manhattan's narrowest house at just over 9ft (3m) wide.

Hudson Street

Retrace your steps on Bedford Street, turn left at Grove Street, and continue one block to Hudson Street. Facing the intersection is the blocky, austere mass of **St Luke in the Fields** ❿, the city's third-oldest church, built in 1822.

Farther up Hudson Street, amid a cluster of boutiques, antique shops, and restaurants, is the **White Horse Tavern** ❻, a favorite of Welsh poet Dylan Thomas before he collapsed here in 1953 after one too many whiskeys. Dylan later died at nearby St Vincent's Hospital.

Bleecker Street

Beyond 11th Street, Hudson Street converges with a six-way intersection around cute and leafy **Abingdon Square** ⓫. This route concludes by heading northwest up Hudson Street to the Meatpacking District, where there are some great options for eat-

Alfresco dining in the hip Meatpacking District

ing. Before making your way there, you could make a detour by turning right on **Bleecker Street,** where you can stroll around the antique shops and boutiques that line the street all the way to Sixth Avenue.

Look, too, for pricey designer shops like **Marc Jacobs** (385 Bleecker), **Mulberry** (387 Bleecker), **Ralph Lauren** (381 Bleecker), and **Juicy Couture** (368 Bleecker), which in the last few years have been cropping up on this strip and elbowing out funky, longtime retailers, much to the consternation of locals.

Bleecker is crossed by some of Greenwich Village's prettiest side streets. Bank Street is particularly lovely, with its cobblestones and pastel houses, as is Perry Street, which is one block farther along.

MEATPACKING DISTRICT

Northwest of Abingdon Square, the Meatpacking District was formerly a neighborhood of meat wholesalers and commercial butchers that has now become one of the city's most fashionable areas.

During the day, you can browse high-end designers; there are a number on **West 14th Street** ⑫ between Ninth and Tenth avenues: **Alexander McQueen** (No. 417), **Jeffrey New York** (No. 449), and Diane Van Furstenberg (at the corner of Washington Street). If you're in need of a break, there's a clutch of restaurants around the cobbled intersection of Hudson,

Gansevoort, and Little West 12th streets where you can stop for dinner or drinks.

It's a fairly laidback scene, and very different from the glitz of the nighttime hours, when thin, rich, and famous celebrities jam the restaurants and nightclubs, flashbulbs pop, and the hoi polloi gawk from behind velvet ropes.

The High Line
At the edge of the Meatpacking District, the High Line runs from Gansevoort to 30th Street between 10th and 11th avenues. This is a defunct, elevated freight railroad transformed into New York's most unusual park. Built in the early 1930s to serve upper-floor loading docks of factories and warehouses, the railroad delivered its last trainload of frozen turkeys in 1980 and was left to molder for 20 years, sprouting a natural garden of wildflowers and weeds. Seeing the potential, a group of friends successfully enlisted the city to save the tracks. The original wild plantings inspired the naturalistic landscaping along a concrete walkway that incorporates parts of the rails and the original metal fencing. It offers seating, and city and Hudson River views from a 30ft (9m) high perspective. There are future plans to extend it further west, as far as the Jacob Javits Center.

Just below the High Line on Washington street, the **Standard Grill** ⑦, has good food and a great terrace.

Strolling along the High Line

Food and Drink

① CAFFE REGGIO

119 MacDougal Street (between Bleecker and West 3rd streets); tel: 212-475-9557; www.cafereggio.com; daily B, L and D; $
Beat poets Allen Ginsberg and Jack Kerouac once hung out here; today you're more likely to find NYU students, but it's still a cozy place to enjoy pastries, panini, pasta, and soups.

② HOME

20 Cornelia Street (between Bleecker and West 4th streets); tel: 212-243-9579; www.homerestaurantnyc.com; Mon–Fri L and D, Sat–Sun Br and D; $$
Home cooking, farm-to-table ingredients and a nice back garden make this cozy spot a local favorite. The lunch menu is served until 4pm.

③ NORTH SQUARE

103 Waverly Place (at McDougal Street); tel: 212-254-1200; www.northsquareny.com; Mon–Fri B, L and D, Sat–Sun B, Br and D; $–$$
A relaxing oasis downstairs in the Washington Square Hotel serving good New American food at keen prices. Good lunch menu with prix-fixe option.

④ ELEPHANT & CASTLE

68 Greenwich Avenue (between Perry and Seventh Avenue); tel: 212-243-1400; Mon–Fri B, L, and D, Sat–Sun Br and D; $
Tiny, sociable old-timer serving sandwiches, salads, burgers, and pub fare, plus a fine Sunday brunch. Try the dessert crepes.

⑤ ROSEMARY'S

18 Greenwich Avenue (near 10th Street); tel: 212-647-1818; rosemarysnyc.com; daily B, L and D; $$
This new enoteca and trattoria boasts a true rooftop garden, where they actually grow some of their ingredients, and is a bright and lively place for small bites and Italian classics.

⑥ WHITE HORSE TAVERN

567 Hudson Street (at West 11th Street); tel: 212-989-3956; daily L and D; $–$$
No bar tour of Greenwich Village is complete without visiting this historic watering hole, a favorite of students and assorted literati ever since Welsh poet Dylan Thomas, following his own advice, pulled up a barstool and went most ungently into that good night.

⑦ STANDARD GRILL

Standard Hotel, 846 Washington Street (at 13th Street); tel: 212-645-4100; www.the standardgrill.com; daily B, L, and D, Sat–Sun Br; $–$$
A unique location below the High Line and an excellent chef serving up American favorites make for a popular addition to the neighborhood. The outdoor terrace is a fine place for a drink at the end of the day.

Bargain goods in Canal Street

SOHO AND TRIBECA

These neighborhoods are the very epitome of post-industrial chic. They are urban playgrounds known the world over for cast-iron architecture, stylish boutiques, loft living, and fantastic food.

DISTANCE: 2.25 miles (3.5km)
TIME: A half- to full day
START: West Broadway
END: Tribeca Film Center
POINTS TO NOTE: The nearest subway stations to the starting point are Prince Street or Spring Street A, C, E. You may wish to build in some time during the tour for shopping in Soho. The tour ends at Tribeca, a great area for dining.

The old industrial neighborhood of Soho (**So**uth of **Ho**uston) was invaded by artists in the 1960s and soon after blossomed into a mecca of avant-garde culture. The artists, however, were soon priced out and most of the galleries have moved on, many of them to Chelsea. Today's neighborhood is devoted far more to shopping than to art.

This tour leads you through a few hot spots, though any number of distractions might lure you off the track. Soho's streets are narrow and the crowds can be daunting, especially on weekends, when many New Yorkers like to brunch and browse, so don't expect to zip through.

WEST BROADWAY

Start your tour at **West Broadway ❶** near Houston Street. West Broadway is Soho's main drag and is lined with high-end boutiques including American giants dkny (No. 420), **Ralph Lauren** (No. 381), and **Eileen Fisher** (No. 395), as well as European designers **Alberta Ferretti** (No. 452) and **Giorgio Armani** (No. 410).

PRINCE STREET

The shopping district spills over into the cross streets, especially **Prince Street ❷**, which hosts **J. Crew** (No. 99), **Miu Miu** (No. 100), **Club Monaco** (No. 121), **Coach** (No. 143), and others.

While you're browsing, take a moment to admire two fine buildings at Prince and Greene streets: **112 Prince Street**, which on its eastern face has an extraordinary *trompe l'œil* mural by artist Richard Haas, and, on the opposite corner, **109 Prince Street**, a handsome

Hanging on a Soho stoop

five-story edifice with a cast-iron facade that houses a Ralph Lauren boutique.

In a former post office a little farther on is Apple's stylish **Station A** (103 Prince Street). Fight your way through the mob to try the latest iPads, iPhones, and other new gadgets. Farther along, at the corner of Mercer Street, is the **Mercer Hotel** (147 Mercer Street; see page 111), a trendy boutique hotel in a beautiful Romanesque Revival building. **Fanelli Café** ➊ is a good nearby eatery to stop at.

GREENE STREET

Retrace your steps to West Broadway and turn left. Browse the shops down to Broome Street, detouring after one block, right down Spring Street, for hot food at **Bistro Les Amis** ➋, if sustenance is required. Turn left at Broome and continue to **Greene Street** ➌. In the late 19th century, this was the center of a notorious red-light district, where brothels conducted business behind shuttered windows. Now the same windows attract a different sort of browser – those who gaze longingly at the latest designs by **Louis Vuitton** (No. 116) and **Hugo Boss** (No. 132).

Soho Historic Cast Iron District
Greene Street is also the heart of the **Soho Historic Cast Iron District**. Most of the structures here were constructed in the mid- to late 1800s,

Cheesey goodness at Dean & Deluca

when manufacturers moved into the neighborhood and needed to create industrial spaces quickly. There was no electricity, of course, so it was necessary for windows to admit a maximum of light. With rear walls often facing gloomy alleys, the only place sunlight could enter was through voluminous front windows. The solution to problems over expense came in the form of buildings with pre-cast iron facades that could be assembled on site. And since casting iron requires less labor than sculpting stone, the facades could be quite ornate.

The prominent **Gunther Building** at the corner of Greene and Broome streets is especially noteworthy. It was built in 1872 as a showroom and warehouse for fur dealer William Gunther and now serves as a collection of loft apartments.

BROADWAY

Take your time exploring Greene Street before returning to Broome Street and walking one block east to **Broadway** ❹. Pause here for a look at the landmark **Haughwout Building** (488–492 Broadway), a palazzo with five stories of arched windows, fluted columns, and prominent cornices, all rendered in cast iron. Built in 1857 for china dealer Eder V. Haughwout, the building was the first to install the newfangled 'safety elevator' invented by Elisha Otis, a development that opened the way for the skyscrapers that would eventually dominate Manhattan's skyline.

Bloomingdale's and around
Despite the presence of a handful of tony stores, Broadway tends to appeal to shoppers with more mainstream tastes than West Broadway. Even smart **Bloomingdale's** (504 Broadway, near Broome Street) caters to young, mid-market customers.

If you're traveling with kids, be sure to stop at **Scholastic Books** (557 Broadway), a huge, colorful retail space opened by the publisher of the Harry Potter series and scores of other well-known children's titles. A few steps away is the landmark **Little Singer Building** (561 Broadway), a 12-story confection of terracotta, steel, and wrought-iron tracery built in 1904

Brightly painted windows mark the entrance to the **Children's Museum of the Arts** (103 Charlton Street, near Greenwich Street; www.cmany.com; Mon and Wed noon–5pm, Thur–Fri noon–6pm, Sat–Sun 10am–5pm; charge), a space that is part museum, part art studio. Here children learn by becoming artists and everything is built half-size.

Across the street, gourmet shop **Dean & Deluca** (560 Broadway) lures foodies from throughout the city. The stand-up coffee bar is a good place for a snack, although the line of caffeine-starved New Yorkers can be fairly long.

Across Prince Street, in a building once occupied by a branch of the Guggenheim Museum, is fashion temple **Prada** ❺ (575 Broadway), which has redesigned the interior in the shape of

Shooting pool in a Tribeca bar

a half-pipe connecting the first and second floors. It's worth a look inside even if you can't afford the merchandise.

TRIBECA

Head back down Broadway for 10 blocks until you reach Leonard Street. In the late 1970s, artists in search of lower rents migrated south from Soho to **Tribeca** (the **Tri**angle **Be**low **Ca**nal). An eclectic blend of renovated warehouses, Corinthian columns, condo towers, and narrow streets, Tribeca's attractions can easily be covered in a morning, leaving lots of time to do what Tribeca does best – indulge in eating. Some of Manhattan's best (and most expensive) bars and restaurants are here, but savvy visitors can soak up the atmosphere at a fraction of the cost by sampling a meal at lunch.

Leonard Street

Some of Tribeca's finest architecture is on **Leonard Street** ❻. Just to the east, the **Clocktower Building** (No. 108) is the former New York Life Insurance Building, remodeled by Stanford White in 1898.

Hudson and Harrison

Leonard ends at Hudson Street. On the corner of Hudson and Harrison is the ornate, recently restored **Mercantile Exchange Building** ❼, built in 1884 as the trading center for the egg and butter business. **Wichcraft**, see ❸, is on the corner of Beach and Greenwich.

Walk half a block west on Harrison, then two blocks north on Greenwich to the **Tribeca Film Center**, the offices of actor Robert De Niro and the hub of the Tribeca Film Festival. Although the center is closed to visitors, you can power lunch in the **Tribeca Grill** (see page 120).

Food and Drink

❶ FANELLI CAFE
94 Prince Street (at Mercer Street); tel: 212-226-9412; daily L, and D; $
This holdover from Soho's industrial past still has the homey vibe of a neighborhood tavern. The kitchen knocks out a great burger.

❷ BISTRO LES AMIS
180 Spring Street (at Thompson Street); tel: 212-226-8645; www.bistrolesamis.

com; daily L and D; $–$$
All the bistro classics plus pastas and salads are served at this friendly longtime neighborhood favourite.

❸ WICHCRAFT
397 Greenwich Street (at Beach Street); 212-780-0577; www.wichcraftnyc.com; daily B and L, early D; $
This handy mini-chain by star chef Tom Colichio (Craft) serves up gourmet sandwiches and paninis, plus a breakfast sandwich all day.

Cakes at Veniero's Pasticceria

EAST VILLAGE AND LOWER EAST SIDE

Take a stroll around St Mark's Place in the East Village, go shopping for new fashions in NoLita, check out the delis and boutiques of the Lower East Side, and take a tour of the Tenement Museum.

DISTANCE: 2.5 miles (4km)
TIME: A half-day
START: St Mark's-in-the-Bowery
END: Orchard Street
POINTS TO NOTE: The best day to do the route is Sunday, when the Orchard Street Market takes place. Whichever day you choose, be sure to book well in advance for the Tenement Museum.

This part of Manhattan is a series of neighborhoods that overlap and bump up next to each other in a convivial and vibrant way. What these areas have shared historically, aside from proximity, is a high-spirited funkiness. Gentrification is changing the mood, however. Today, these neighborhoods boast a growing number of top restaurants and boutiques that appeal to the young and hip. If you wish to fortify yourself with coffee and cake before exploring, try **Veniero's Pasticceria**, see ❶, a short walk from the starting point on East 11th Street.

EAST VILLAGE

The route starts in the **East Village**, which, even after years of gentrification, still has a bit of raw bohemian quality. In the late 1960s, this was the epicenter of East Coast counterculture, where Andy Warhol presented Velvet Underground 'happenings' and the scene at nightclubs like the infamous Electric Circus were heavily seasoned with psychedelic lights and hallucinogens.

But the East Village is much older than this. The church of **St Mark's-in-the-Bowery ❶**, where this route begins, was built in 1799 on land that belonged to Peter Stuyvesant, the last Dutch governor of New York. Stuyvesant is buried in a nearby cemetery.

Cooper Square

At the end of Stuyvesant Street you will emerge onto **Cooper Square**. Ahead is an immense brownstone structure, **Cooper Union ❷**, established by inventor and entrepreneur Peter Cooper in 1859 as a college for the underprivileged. Abraham Lincoln made his

Astor Place   *Salamis at Katz's Delicatessen*

famous 'Might Makes Right' speech here in 1860, cementing his bid for the presidential nomination. The high-rise **Cooper Square Hotel** that appeared here recently is a very tangible sign of gentrification.

St Mark's Place

Turn around and head along the East Village's 'main street,' **St Mark's Place** ❸.The attitude here is a good-natured mix of punk, funk, and radical politics. Sidewalk cafés heave with customers, and the bazaar-like atmosphere is augmented by street vendors. Bars and restaurants are plentiful and filled with local characters; for years they have been hanging out one block south at **McSorley's Old Ale House**, see ❷.

Just by Tompkins Square Park is **Alphabet City**, so named because of its avenues A, B, C, and D. Once known for crime and poverty, many of its slums have been replaced by restaurants and bars that attract a hip young crowd.

Public Theater

From McSorley's turn right and cross Cooper Square. A few steps north on Fourth Avenue is **Astor Place** ❹, where there is a handsome cast-iron subway kiosk, as well as a black cube by Tony Rosenthal called *The Alamo.*

Walk south on Lafayette Street to the **Public Theater** ❺, headquartered in the majestic Astor Library, and built in the late 19th century. The theater is devoted to both Shakespeare and new plays, some of which have become major hits, like *Hair* and *A Chorus Line.*

Buzzy Little Italy streets

NOLITA AND LITTLE ITALY

Continue four blocks south on Lafayette to East Houston Street. The area just south of Houston is a fun, savvy, boutique-laden lair known as **NoLita**. **Mulberry Street** ⑥ is the heart of this temple to trendy retail, and there are lots of watering holes and restaurants in the surrounding side streets.

St Patrick's Old Cathedral ⑦ was the seat of the Catholic archdiocese until 1879, when the 'new' St Patrick's Cathedral on Fifth Avenue was completed. Services were held in Italian, highlighting the fact that this part of the city was in **Little Italy** ⑧.

Although NoLita (**No**rth of **Li**ttle **Ita**ly) and **Chinatown** farther south have both encroached upon its borders, Little Italy is still an atmospheric place for a meal, especially during the Feast of San Gennaro, the annual 10-day event which is held during the September.

LOWER EAST SIDE

The Lower East Side, which slants south of East Houston Street to the East River, is where Jewish immigrants from Eastern Europe settled toward the end of the 19th century. In and around the early 20th century, this was the most densely populated place in the world, with as many as 1,000 people per acre on its mean streets.

These days you'll see Chinese or Hispanic stores that, despite retaining Jewish names, demonstrate that the neighborhood still attracts new arrivals. Lately these have included trendy young New Yorkers, and with them, the advent of the fashionable boutiques, bars, and hotels that thrive around Orchard, Ludlow, and Rivington streets.

The Bowery

East of NoLita and Little Italy is the **Bowery** ⑨, a long north–south street that gave this section of the Lower East Side its name. For years considered Manhattan's Skid Row, even this notoriously

---

Traditional eats

No tour of the Lower East Side is complete without visiting a few of the neighborhood's delis, bakeries, and candy shops. Tank up for a long day of walking at Yonah Schimmel Bakery (137 East Houston St), where knishes – mounds of dough stuffed with potato, spinach, or kasha – are baked in a brick oven. A few doors away, you can pick up paper-thin lox (smoked salmon), caviar, and herring at Russ & Daughters (179 E. Houston). Around the corner, Economy Candy (108 Rivington St) has been satisfying New York's sweet tooth since the 1930s. If you're near the Tenement Museum, try ice cream at Il Laboratorio del Gelato (95 Orchard St) or a salty, garlicky pickle at The Pickle Guys (49 Essex St). Just around the block, Kossar's Bialys (367 Grand St) offers up bagels and warm, pliant bialys (onion rolls).

In the Lower East Side Tenement Museum

seedy strip is getting the Soho treatment, as posh nightclubs, designer shops, and million-dollar lofts open amid former flophouses and whiskey joints.

Underscoring this gentrification is the **New Museum of Contemporary Art** ❿ (No. 235 Bowery at Prince Street; www.newmuseum.org; Wed–Sun 11am–6pm, Thur until 9pm; charge) showing avant-garde work by living artists.

Tenement Museum

From the art museum head south two blocks and turn left onto Delancey Street. Five blocks along is Orchard Street where, on the corner at No. 108, you will find the visitor centre for the **Lower East Side Tenement Museum** ⓫ (www.tenement.org; tours daily; charge). The museum is a thematic tour of an actual 1863 tenement building at No. 97. Over a span of seven decades this one building housed more than 7,000 people from some 20 countries. The building can only be seen by guided tour; these book up in advance and times vary, so call ahead or check the website for reservations. A limited number of same-day tickets are available at the visitor center.

Orchard Street to Houston

The best way to get further acquainted with this neighborhood is to walk up Orchard Street from the museum to Houston Street. If possible, visit on Sunday, when it is at its busiest (many stores are closed Friday afternoon and Saturday in observance of the Jewish Sabbath).

Once crowded with peddlers selling cut-rate clothing, **Orchard Street** today offers some discount designer fashions, but the old shops are giving way to quirky boutiques and vintage clothes shops, some with backroom art galleries. There are also several cool cafés, including the legendary **Katz's Delicatessen** ❸.

Food and Drink

❶ VENIERO'S PASTICCERIA

342 East 11th Street (near First Avenue); tel: 212-674-7070; www.venierospastry.com; Sun–Thur 8am–12am, Fri–Sat 8am–1am; $
A classic Italian pastry shop and café founded in 1894.

❷ MCSORLEY'S OLD ALE HOUSE

15 East 7th Street (near Third Avenue); tel: 212-474-9148; Mon–Sat 11am–1am, Sun 1pm–1am; $
In business since the 1850s, this classic New York saloon still has sawdust on the floors.

❸ KATZ'S DELICATESSEN

205 East Houston Street (at Ludlow Street); tel: 212-254-2246; katzsdelicatessen.com; daily B, L, and D; $$
This Jewish deli is a New York institution, and the huge space is often filled to capacity. You might recognize it from the famous fake orgasm scene in the film *When Harry Met Sally*.

New York's skyline from the river

LOWER MANHATTAN

A tour of the Financial District, taking in the New York Stock Exchange, Federal Hall, Trinity Church, the 9/11 Memorial, and Battery Park, plus a walk along the Hudson River and a visit to the enduring South Street Seaport.

DISTANCE: 2.45 miles (4km)
TIME: A full day
START: Stock Exchange
END: South Street Seaport
POINTS TO NOTE: While this route could easily take a full day, you may wish to do the first half in the morning, including lunch at the World Financial Center, and then catch a ferry from Battery Park in the afternoon either to the Statue of Liberty and Ellis Island, or to Staten Island (route 16).

Lower Manhattan is the original New York, where winding streets lead to busy, international docks. Today, these narrow byways are lined by towering temples of finance, museums, elegant churches, and, on the eastern side, South Street Seaport, a complex of historic waterfront buildings, ships, dining, and shops.

Start this tour in the heart of the Financial District: outside the imposing neoclassical temple that houses the **New York Stock Exchange ❶** on Broad Street just a few steps from Wall Street.

Inside, the trading floor is a frenzy of buying and selling that, for better or worse, underpins the American economy.

WALL STREET

Walk to the corner of Wall Street and turn right for **Federal Hall ❷** (26 Wall Street; www.nps.gov/feha; Mon–Fri 9am–5pm, some Sats in summer; free), a Greek Revival edifice built in 1842 on what was the site of the British City Hall. George Washington was inaugurated as the country's first president here in 1789. Inside are free exhibits focusing on American history with an emphasis on the role of New York City and its many prominent residents.

Anyone keen on history may also want to investigate the **Museum of American Finance ❸** (48 Wall Street; www.moaf.org; Tue–Sat 10am–4pm; charge), housed in the former Bank of New York headquarters, near Federal Hall.

Trinity Church

Double back on Wall Street about three blocks to Broadway, where the Gothic

A famous address   *Trinity Church*

bell tower of **Trinity Church** ❹ rises up like an exclamation point. Surrounding the church are some of the city's oldest graves.

Just north of Fulton street, sits **St Paul's Chapel** ❺ (209 Broadway), the city's oldest church, built in 1766. A more modest space than Trinity Church, St Paul's reflects the earlier Georgian style of architecture, and it too has a peaceful graveyard that is the final resting place of many early city residents.

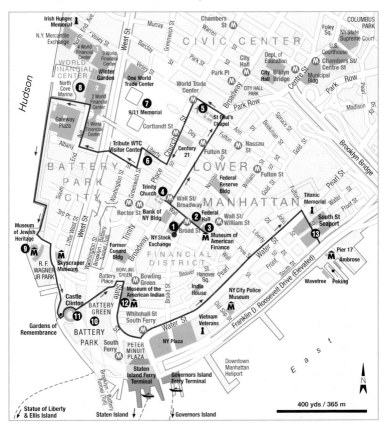

WORLD TRADE CENTER SITE

The church borders Vesey Street on the northern end. Follow Vesey one block west and turn left onto Church Street, passing under the shadow of 1,776-foot-tall **One World Center**. Turn right on Liberty Street for a visit to the **Tribute WTC Visitor Center** ❻ (120 Liberty Street; www.tributewtc. org; Mon–Sat 10am–6pm, Sun 10am–5pm; suggested donation). This non-profit organization was set up in the aftermath of the September 11, 2001 tragedy to allow those most affected to stay in touch. A documentary on life before the attack has testimonies from former employees and local residents, while other galleries focus on events as they unfolded, and the rescue and clean-up operation.

A block south on Greenwich Street you will come upon the entrance to the **9/11 Memorial** ❼ (Greenwich and Albany streets; www.911memorial.org; daily mid-Sep–mid-Mar 10am–6pm, mid-Mar–mid-Sep 10am–8pm, last entry one hour before closing; free). Appropriately tranquil and somber, the outdoor memorial welcomes a select number of visitors per day (reserve tickets online or pick them up near St Paul's Chapel at 20 Vesey Street) so that everyone has sufficient time and space to pay tribute to the victims of the country's worst terrorist attack. Deep reflective waterfalls and pools sit in the footprints of the two fallen towers. Names of the nearly 3,000 who died are etched into the walls of the pool. When the accompanying museum opens, there will be multi-media and interactive exhibitions.

WORLD FINANCIAL CENTER

Exit at the corner of Albany and West streets and head toward the Hudson River. Turn right on South End Avenue and follow it to the **World Financial Center** ❽. Here, a few shops and restaurants are clustered around the **Winter Garden**, a marble plaza with palm trees under a vaulted glass roof. Take the opportunity to eat barbecue at **Blue Smoke** ❶, or go healthy and stock up on energy at the **Elixir Juice Bar** ❷.

HUDSON RIVER ESPLANADE

It's about a 10-minute walk south along the river **Esplanade** to the **Museum of Jewish Heritage** ❾ (36 Battery Place; www.mjhnyc.org; Sun–Thur 10am–5.45pm, Wed until 8pm, Fri 10am–3pm; charge). The museum lies by the spot where Jews first set foot in North America in 1654. Exhibits draw from a rich pool of personal artifacts to present the story of the Jewish people and put the Holocaust into the context of 20th-century history.

Battery Park

Follow Battery Place to **Battery Park** ❿ at Manhattan's southern tip. Encompassed within its 21 acres (8 hectares)

A space for reflection at the 9/11 Memorial

are gardens, walkways, and monuments, including a spherical bronze sculpture that was salvaged from the rubble of the World Trade Center Plaza and re-installed here as a 9/11 memorial. It's called *An Icon of Hope*.

At the water's edge is **Castle Clinton** ⑪, a stone fort built as a defense against the British during the run-up to the War of 1812 and later used as a theater and immigration station. It now serves as the ticket office for the **Statue of Liberty and Ellis Island ferries** (see page 94).

Bowling Green

Across State Street from Battery Park is the **National Museum of the American Indian** ⑫ (1 Bowling Green, www.nmai.si.edu; daily 10am–5pm, Thur until 8pm; free), housed in the ornate Beaux Arts Custom House designed by Cass Gilbert in the early 1900s. The museum showcases highlights from a vast collection of Native American art held by the Smithsonian Institution.

The museum fronts a cobbled plaza known as **Bowling Green**, New York's oldest public park and site of the massive 7,000lb (3,000kg) bronze *Charging Bull*, created in 1989 by Arturo Di Modica. It is commonly believed among stockbrokers that rubbing a certain part of the bull's anatomy brings good luck to the market.

SOUTH STREET SEAPORT

From Bowling Green, State Street loops around past Whitehall Street and the

Staten Island Ferry Terminal to Water Street, where you can either hail a cab, hop on a bus, or walk about 10 blocks to Fulton Street, then right to the **South Street Seaport** ⑬ (12–14 Fulton Street; www.southstreetseaport.com; Pier 17 only, currently Mon–Sat 10am–10pm, Sun 11am–10pm; free). Unfrtunately, flooding from Hurricane Sandy damaged many of the piers, galleries and businesses located here and much of it is undergoing renovation or demolition, making way for a new version of the seaport, set to open in 2015. Some shops on Pier 17, however, will continue to operate through the renovations.

Food and Drink

① BLUE SMOKE
World Financial Center, 255 Vesey Street; tel: 212-889-2005; daily L and D; $$
An upscale entry in New York's constantly evolving barbecue scene and a popular lunch spot for traders. It's a good choice for a quick, tasty and filling sit-down meal.

② ELIXIR JUICE BAR
Two World Financial Center, 225 Liberty Street; tel: 212-945-0400; www.elixirjuice.com; daily 7am–7pm; $
The smoothies at this takeout place are practically a meal in themselves, and, according to the owners, can help cure a wide variety of afflictions.

Lady Liberty

STATUE OF LIBERTY AND ELLIS ISLAND

Stop for coffee and pastries near Wall Street, then board the ferry to the monumental statue and historic building that received more than 12 million new arrivals during the great age of American immigration.

DISTANCE: 3 miles (5km)
TIME: A half-day
START: Stone Street
END: Battery Park
POINTS TO NOTE: Ferries to the Statue of Liberty and Ellis Island depart from Battery Park in Lower Manhattan every hour minutes from approximately 8am to 2pm (seasonal variations). Tickets can be bought at Castle Clinton or online at www.statuecruises.com (tel: 201-604-2800 for more information). Free park-ranger-led tours of both islands are conducted daily. To climb to the Statue of Liberty crown, a pass is required; these are available at www.statuecruises.com.

This route's first port of call is **Financier Patisserie** ❶, on **Stone Street**, for coffee and pastries to set you up for the day. Once sated, head south to **Battery Park** ❶, for the ferry to the Statue of Liberty.

STATUE OF LIBERTY

The **Statue of Liberty** ❷ (Liberty Island; www.nps.gov/stli; ferries daily approx. 8am–2pm; charge), or to give her full name, *Liberty Enlightening the World*, was a gift from the people of France, and was conceived by Edouard-René Lefebvre de Laboulaye, a Gallic admirer of American democracy.

De Laboulaye conveyed his enthusiasm to sculptor Frédéric-Auguste Bartholdi, who not only designed the monument but took a leading role in raising funds for its construction. The engineer Gustave Eiffel, who would later gain enduring renown for his eponymous tower erected for the 1889 World Fair, designed the trusswork that supports the copper skin.

The statue was completed in France in July 1884, and arrived in New York Harbor in June 1885 on board the French frigate *Isère*. In transit, Lady Liberty and her crown, torch, tablet, and other accessories were reduced to 350 pieces and packed in 214 crates. It took four months to reassemble the statue in its entirety. On October 28 1886, a dedication by President Grover Cleveland took place in front of thousands of spectators.

Faces of immigration at Ellis Island

ELLIS ISLAND

After visiting the statue, the ferry traditionally continues to **Ellis Island ❸**, which was for 62 years, from 1892 to 1954, the gateway to the United States, and known as the 'Island of Tears,' because of the stress caused to applicants by the strict medical, mental, and literacy tests imposed. Today, more than 100 million Americans are descendants of the around 12 million immigrants who landed at Ellis Island in search of a better life.

Immigration Museum

Allowed to fall into ruin after it was closed in 1954, the main building on the island was restored with $156 million in private funds, and in 1990 reopened as the **Ellis Island Immigration Museum** (www.ellisisland.org; ferries as for Statue of Liberty; charge) chronicling the island's history. At the time of this writing, Ellis Island was closed due to extensive damage suffered during Hurricane Sandy. A reopening date has not been announced, but when it does reopen, exhibits will include photographs, artifacts, personal papers, and audio recordings that recreate the process of entering the country.

After your tour of at least the statue, take time to enjoy the views of the Manhattan skyline, before catching a ferry back to the mainland.

STATEN ISLAND FERRY

The **Staten Island Ferry ❹** may be the best tourist deal in New York. The free, 20-minute ferry shuttles passengers between the Whitehall Terminal adjacent to Battery Park and St George Terminal on Staten Island. Views of the Statue of Liberty and Lower Manhattan are excellent. The panorama is especially inspiring after dark.

Food and Drink

❶ FINANCIER PATISSERIE

62 Stone Street (at Mill Lane); tel: 212-344-5600; www.financierpastries.com; Mon–Sat B and L; $

Start the day with coffee and a choice of tarts, croissants, and other pastries at this delightful café on a cobbled side street closed to traffic. Lunch is nice, too, with soups, salads, and hot-press sandwiches. Outdoor tables shaded with umbrellas give the patisserie an authentic Parisian feel.

The Brooklyn Bridge looms large

BROOKLYN

Catch a subway train to the suburbs and unwind with the Brooklynites in Prospect Park, which is home to Brooklyn Botanic Garden and the wonderfully eclectic Brooklyn Museum of Art.

> **DISTANCE:** 1.5 miles (2.5km)
> **TIME:** A half- to full day
> **START/END:** Grand Army Plaza
> **POINTS TO NOTE:** This route focuses on the Prospect Park area of Brooklyn. To get to the starting point take the 2 or 3 train to Grand Army Plaza. If you want to spend longer in Brooklyn, consider a walk across the Brooklyn Bridge and/or a visit to one of the borough's many neighborhoods, such as Brooklyn Heights or DUMBO.

Brooklyn is the city's most populated borough, connected to Lower Manhattan by the striking **Brooklyn Bridge**. Opened in 1883, it was called the 'eighth wonder of the world.'

Brooklyn has many neighborhoods, some dating from the borough's days of Dutch occupancy in the 1600s. One area that is always desirable is **Brooklyn Heights**; the Brooklyn Heights Promenade has handsome townhouses on one side and views of Manhattan and the East River on the other.

When Soho became too expensive, artists moved over the water to lofts in **DUMBO** (Down Under the Manhattan Bridge Overpass), then to Williamsburg and Red Hook. Any of these areas is worth an afternoon's visit, strolling around the galleries and shops.

PROSPECT PARK

Start at **Grand Army Plaza ❶**, a monumental square with a triumphal arch that serves as the entrance to 585-acre (237-hectare) **Prospect Park**. The park was designed in 1866 by Frederick Law Olmsted and Calvert Vaux and is thought by many to exceed their achievement in Central Park, which they designed eight years earlier. A short walk leads into **Long Meadow ❷**, a mile of gently sloping grassland where Brooklynites come to picnic, play ball, and generally unwind.

BOTANIC GARDEN

Return to Grand Army Plaza and a short walk east on Eastern Parkway leads

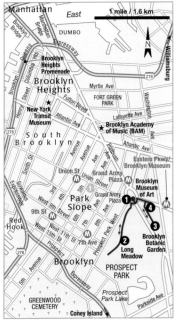

Grand Army Plaza

Cherry blossom at Brooklyn Botanical Gardens

to the **Brooklyn Botanic Garden** ❸ (www.bbg.org; Tue–Fri 8am–4.30pm, Sat–Sun 10am–4.30pm, extended summer hours; charge), which is made up of 52 acres (21 hectares) of specialty gardens, with a program of concerts and festivals.

BROOKLYN MUSEUM OF ART

Also accessible from Eastern Parkway is the **Brooklyn Museum of Art** ❹ (www.brooklynmuseum.org; Wed–Sun 11am–6pm, Thur until 10pm; charge), second only to the Metropolitan as New York City's largest. There are 28 period rooms and an unsual outdoor sculpture garden. Scholars and art fans from all over the world come here to study the museum's respected Egyptian collection.

Every first Saturday of the month, Brooklyn Museum extends its opening hours until 11pm. With free admission, plus lively music and dance shows in the lobby, and wine served in the late-closing Museum Café, there's quite a buzz.

For more low-key daily refreshment, however, try the aforementioned café, or the one at the Botanic Garden, but there are some great alternative dinner and brunch options nearby, such as **Rose Water** ❶. Return to Grand Army Plaza and take Union Street three blocks northwest.

Food and Drink

❶ ROSE WATER

787 Union Street; tel: 718-783 3800; www.rosewaterrestaurant.com; Mon–Fri D, Sat–Sun Br and D; $$–$$$

With a dinky dining room and sheltered terrace, Rose Water does seasonal American food, with the focus on quality organic ingredients. The weekend prix-fixe brunch menu of eggs, waffles, and French toast is popular with locals.

In New York City Botanical Garden

THE BRONX

Take a day trip to the Bronx for a stroll through one of the world's premier botanical centers, a tour of the country's largest urban zoo, and dinner in New York's 'other' Little Italy.

DISTANCE: 3 miles (5km)
TIME: A half- to full day
START: Botanical Garden Station
END: Fordham Road Station
POINTS TO NOTE: Take the Metro–North Harlem local line from Grand Central Terminal to Botanical Garden Station. The journey takes 20 minutes (see www.mta.info). To return to Grand Central from Arthur Avenue, walk to Fordham Road Station (417 East Fordham Road at Third Avenue). The garden is closed Mondays and selected zoo attractions are closed in winter when some animals hibernate.

Food and Drink

① DOMINICK'S

2335 Arthur Avenue (at 187th Street); tel: 718-733-2807; daily L and D; $$
Fans claim that this is the real Little Italy. There's no menu – the waiter tells you all you need – and no check: they just size you up and name a figure.

In 1641 a Scandinavian, Jonas Bronck, bought 500 acres (200 hectares) of virgin forest from Native Americans. The Indian land was called Keskeskeck, but was soon known as 'Bronck's Land.' Part of the original hemlock forest remains in Bronx Park, which includes the two attractions covered here.

BOTANICAL GARDEN

From the Botanical Garden station walk across Kazimiroff Boulevard to the Mosholu Gate of the **New York Botanical Garden ①** (www.nybg.org; Apr–Oct Tue–Sun 10am–6pm, Nov–Mar Tue–Sun 10am–5pm, and holiday Mondays; charge). There are more than 40 specialty gardens, especially attractive in spring. The **Enid A. Haupt Conservatory** is a highlight, a crystal palace with a Palm Court and greenhouses constructed in 1902. The **Rockefeller Rose Garden** is a vision not to be missed in late May–early June, and the **Everett Children's Adventure Garden** has pint-size topiaries and mazes that make for hours of fun for youngsters.

Gorilla at Bronx Zoo *Head to Arthur Avenue for an Italian meal*

BRONX ZOO

The **Bronx Zoo** ❷ (Bronx River Parkway and Fordham Road; www.bronxzoo.com; Apr–Oct Mon–Fri 10am–5pm, Sat–Sun 10am–5.30pm, Nov–Mar daily 10am–4.30pm; charge) is a 20-minute walk away. Exit the Botanical Garden from Conservatory Gate, turn left down Kazimiroff Boulevard, cross Fordham Road and walk along Southern Boulevard to the pedestrian entrance on your left.

This is the largest metropolitan zoo in the US and home to around 4,500 animals. The attractions include a monorail ride over Wild Asia (home to Asian elephants, antelopes, and rhinoceros), a 40-acre (16-hectare) complex with moats to keep the big cats away from their prey (ie the spectators), and the Congo Gorilla Forest, 6.5 acres (2.5 hectares) of forest and bamboo thickets. There's also a sealion pool, bison range, and children's zoo, as well as indoor facilities for nocturnal animals, reptiles, monkeys, and more.

LITTLE ITALY

Take a cab to end your tour with an Italian meal at **Dominick's** ❶ in the **Belmont** neighborhood, the Bronx's Little Italy, around **Arthur Avenue** ❸ and East 187th Street (which joins the Southern Boulevard).

DIRECTORY

Hand-picked hotels and restaurants to suit all budgets and tastes, organised by area, plus select nightlife listings, an alphabetical listing of practical information and an overview of the best books and films to give you a flavour of the city.

Room at Casablanca Hotel

ACCOMMODATIONS

New York hotels are the most expensive in the US and you may not get much space for your money, but some recent additions have made the city a bit more affordable. The five-star properties are as luxurious as any in the world, although tabs beginning at $600 a day will be beyond many travelers. The listings below feature a wider range of choices. Rates vary by season, with the low periods in winter and in August, but hotel websites may have special rates and packages at anytime. Many hotels offer discounts for longer stays or reservations booked well in advance. Discount websites are useful as well; www.quikbook.com has many New York offerings; www.kayak.com lets you compare several services on one site. Added to your hotel bill will be city, state, and occupancy taxes of 14.75% percent plus a room charge of $2 per night.

Students and other budget travelers might consider staying at one of several hostels. Most offer dorm-style lodging, shared bathrooms, and a common kitchen for a fraction of the cost of a standard hotel. Manhattan locations include Big Apple Hostel (119 West 45th Street; tel: 212-302-2603; www.bigapplehostel.com); Chelsea International Hostel (251 West 20th Street; tel: 212-243-7700; www.chelseahostel.com); and HI-New York (891 Amsterdam Avenue; tel: 212-932-2300; http://hinewyork.org). Or of course, there's always the trusty YMCA (six locations; tel: 917-441-8800; www.ymcanyc.org/association/guest-rooms)

Bed and breakfast accommodations in New York range from a room in someone's apartment to a full apartment or small inn. For information, contact City Lights (tel: 212-737-7049; www.citylightsnewyork.com) or Bed and Breakfast Network of New York (tel: 212-645-8134, 800-900-8134; http://bedandbreakfastnetny.com).

Midtown

414 Hotel

414 West 46th Street (between Ninth and Tenth avenues); tel: 212-399-0006; www.414hotel.com; subway: 42nd Street Eighth Avenue; $$

Two brownstones with a courtyard between them have been transformed into a best-bet budget boutique with a location that is perfect for Broadway theaters.

Price for a double room for one night without breakfast:
$$$$ = over $300
$$$ = $250–$300
$$ = $200–$250
$ = under $200

The Iroquois New York

The Benjamin

125 East 50th Street (at Lexington Avenue); tel: 212-715-2500, 1866-222-2365; www.thebenjamin.com; subway: 51st Street; $$$

One of New York City's boutique-style hotels, the Benjamin offers business and leisure travelers four-star amenities and some of the most comfortable beds in New York, at relatively reasonable prices. Rooms have galley kitchens with a microwave and fridge, and some have terraces. There is also a spa, fitness center, restaurant, and cocktail lounge. The lovely Art Deco building was erected in 1927, the work of world-renowned architect Emery Roth.

Casablanca Hotel

147 West 43rd Street (6th Avenue and Broadway); tel: 212-869-1212, 888-922-7225; www.casablancahotel.com; subway: Times Square 42nd Street; $$$

Wonderful, small hotels are rare in New York, yet here is a lovely and inviting choice. The décor throughout evokes Morocco, with Murano glass hallway sconces and beautifully tiled and appointed bathrooms. Continental breakfast included.

Distrikt Hotel

342 West 40th Street (at Ninth Avenue); tel: 212-706-6100, 888-444-5610; http://distrikthotel.com; subway: 42nd Street Broadway or Eighth Avenue; $$

A sleek boutique Theater District newcomer with a twist – each floor has a city neighbourhood theme. Amenities are luxury (Frette linens, robes, soundproof windows) but rates are not.

Dylan Hotel

52 East 41st Street (at Madison Avenue); tel: 212-338 0500; www.dylanhotel.com; subway: Grand Central 42nd Street; $$

A small, sleek, upscale boutique hotel at reasonable prices, centrally located blocks away from Grand Central Terminal. Housed in a 1903 Beaux Arts building once home to a chemists' society.

Hotel Edison

228 West 47th Street (at Broadway); tel: 212-840 5000; www.edisonhotelnyc.com; subway: 49th Street; $$

Hotels in the bottom price ranges hardly ever really stand out, but the Edison is an exception. Though the Art Deco lobby can be chaotic, the rooms in this huge hotel are quite comfortable, pleasantly if simply decorated, and quiet. May be the best deal in NYC.

The Iroquois New York

49 West 44th Street (5th and 6th avenues); tel: 212-840-3080, 800-332-7220; www.iroquoisny.com; subway: Times Square 42nd Street; $$$$

This luxurious boutique hotel is close enough to the theater district to be convenient but far enough away to be out of the path of most of the crowds. Standard rooms are not large, but they accommodate a king-size bed without

The library at Hotel Metro

feeling too cramped. The health club is first-rate.

The London NYC

151 West 54th Street (between Sixth and Seventh avenues); tel: 866-690-2029; www.thelondonnyc.com; subway: Seventh Avenue; $$$

The all-suite London boasts style and unusually large quarters for New York, not to mention room service from the first NY outpost of London star chef Gordon Ramsay.

The Mansfield

12 West 44th Street (at 5th Avenue); tel: 212-277 8700, 800-255 5167; www.mansfieldhotel.com; subway: Fifth Avenue; $$

Less expensive than the Algonquin and the Royalton hotels, which are located on the same street, this intimate, elegant boutique-style hotel mixes old-world style (the building dates from 1903) with modern details. Rooms are small, but the quality and the service are high. The Mansfield is one of those places that happy, satisfied guests return to on subsequent visits to New York City.

Hotel Metro

45 West 35th Street (between Fifth and Sixth avenues); tel: 212-947-2500; www.hotelmetronyc.com; subway: 34th Street Herald Square; $$

Popular with the fashion industry, the Metro has a Deco feel, spacious rooms that are updated regularly, and nice features like a library, rooftop terrace, and free continental breakfast.

Michelangelo Hotel

152 West 51st Street (just west of Seventh Avenue); tel: 212-765-1900; www.michelangelohotel.com; subway: 49th Street N or R, 50th Street 1; $$–$$$

An oasis of calm and elegance just off Broadway, this hotel offers old-world ambience and comfortable rooms at comfortable rates.

New York Palace

455 Madison Avenue (at 50th Street); tel: 212-888 7000, 800-804-7035; www.new yorkpalace.com; subway: 5th Avenue 53rd Street; $$$

A grandiose monument to lavish pomp and excess and appointed in a style that can only be called postmodern Rococo, the Palace has a regime of flawlessly detailed service to make the average guest feel like an imperial pasha.

The Paramount

235 West 46th Street (at Broadway and 8th Avenue); tel: 212-764 5500, 877-692 0803; www.nycparamount.com; subway: 49th Street; $$

A mix of retro and contemporary in the heart of Times Square. The rooms and public spaces pay homage to the theater design of the 1920s but through a modern and minimalist lens: amenities include extravagant 'entertainment suites,' access to the hotel's iPads and

The Plaza's Palm Court

In the Plaza's Fitzgerald Suite

iMacs, and a classic theater district bar. Rooms are small but well equipped.

Le Parker Meridien

119 West 56th Street (at 6th Avenue); tel: 212-245 5000, 800-543 4300; www.parker meridien.com; subway: 57th Street; $$$

Part of the internationally known French chain: modern, airy, with an excellent restaurant, Norma's (known for its great breakfast), a bar with one of the city's best burgers, health facilities that include a swimming pool, and a barbershop.

Peninsula New York

700 Fifth Ave (at 55th Street); tel: 212-956 2888; www.peninsula.com; subway: Fifth Avenue West 53rd Street; $$$$

One of the city's most lavish hotels, where richly appointed rooms go for about $750 (slightly less with corporate rates). The hotel's health club and spa are truly luxurious. It's also in a prime location on Fifth Avenue and has a wonderful rooftop bar.

The Plaza

Fifth Avenue (at 59th Street); tel: 212-759-3000; www.theplazany.com; subway: Fifth Avenue; $$$

One of New York's grand hotels, The Plaza recently underwent a renovation that restored its Edwardian-style splendor. Rooms are furnished with antiques and adorned with murals. The Oak Bar and the Rose Club are favorite pre- and post-theater spots.

La Quinta Manhattan

17 West 32nd Street (near Fifth Avenue); tel: 212-736-1600, 800-567-7720; www.applecorehotels.com; subway: 34th Street Herald Square; $

Like others in the Apple Core Hotels group, rates at this 182-room hotel, a short walk from Macy's and Madison Square Garden, are extremely reasonable, especially considering that the comfortable rooms come with free wifi and continental breakfast. There's also a lobby cafe with entertainment, a restaurant with room service, and – rare in this price category – an open-air rooftop bar where music and snacks can be enjoyed in summer, along with views of the Empire State Building.

The Royalton

44 West 44th Street (at 5th and 6th avenues); tel: 212-869 4400; www.royalton hotel.com; subway: Times Square 42nd Street; $$$

Another chic and ultra-modern creation from Ian Schrager of Studio 54 fame. Every line and appointment – from the lobby to the lavatories – is as boldly, coldly futuristic as the set of a sci-fi film, complete with video and stereo gadgetry. Still, the Royalton bends over backwards to provide the scurrying, 'can-do' pampering expected by its clientele. Handy for the theater district.

St Regis

2 East 55th Street (at 5th Avenue); tel:

A Grand Suite at the St Regis

212-753 4500; www.stregisnewyork.com; subway: Fifth Avenue 53rd Street; $$$$

A grand Edwardian wedding cake of a building, filigreed and charmingly muraled (by the likes of Maxfield Parrish). The St Regis is a magnet for somewhat older, moneyed guests who appreciate the ambience of a more regal age. The location doesn't hurt; nor does the legendary King Cole Bar.

Waldorf-Astoria

50th Street and Park Avenue; tel: 212-355-3000, 800-925-3673; www.waldorf.com; subway: 51st Street 6; $$$$

The most famous hotel in the city during its heyday in the 1930s and 1940s, with a panache that's been restored to something like its early glory. Most rooms have an old-world charm, and the location is convenient.

Wellington Hotel

871 Seventh Avenue (at 55th Street); tel: 212-247-3900, 800-652-1212; www.wellingtonhotel.com; subway: 57th Street F; $$

The side-street entrance in a congested neighborhood is useful and the location is great for Central Park, Lincoln Center, and Carnegie Hall. A reliable standby for reasonable rates.

W New York

541 Lexington Avenue (near East 49th Street); tel: 212-755-1200; www.wnewyork.com; subway: 51st Street 6; $$$

W's interior was designed by entertainment architect David Rockwell and features Zen-inspired rooms. There's a juice bar, a spa with good fitness facilities, and a trendsetting restaurant called Heartbeat.

Chelsea to Gramercy Park

70 Park Avenue

70 Park Avenue (at 38th Street); tel: 212-973-2400, 877-707-2752; www.70parkave.com: subway: Grand Central; $$

Reasonable rates are a nice surprise at this classy Park Avenue boutique hotel that feels almost like your own pied-à-terre. Rooms are well appointed, and there's a complimentary wine reception in the lobby every night.

Ace Hotel

20 West 29th Street (at Broadway); tel: 212-679-2222; www.acehotel.com/newyork; subway: 28th Street R; $$$

The former Breslin Hotel boasts a hip clientele, a celebrated restaurant and stylish rooms. Too bad there isn't much to do in the surrounding neighborhood.

Gershwin Hotel

7 East 27th Street (at 5th Avenue); tel: 212-545 8000; www.gershwinhotel.com; subway: 28th Street; $$

An artsy hotel just north of Madison Square Park inspired by Andy Warhol and aimed at the young, fashionable, and cash-strapped. Temporary art exhibits in the lobby.

The Ace Hotel's lobby

Gramercy Park Hotel

2 Lexington Avenue (at Gramercy Park); tel: 212-920-3300; www.gramercyparkhotel. com; subway: 23rd Street 6; $$$$

Once a faded relic from the Jazz Age, this property was brought back to life as a swank boutique hotel adorned with rich velvets, modern art, and chandeliers. The Rose and Jade bars are favorite celebrity hangouts.

Hampton Inn Chelsea

108 West 24th Street (at 6th Avenue); tel: 212-414 1000; www.hamptoninn.com; subway: 23rd Street; $

Hi-tech decor sets the tone at this Chelsea spot situated at the doorstep of the gallery scene. Great location for shopping on nearby Sixth Avenue.

Inn at Irving Place

56 Irving Place (near East 18th Street); tel: 212-533-4600, 800-685-1447; www.innatirving.com; subway: 23rd Street 6; $$$$

This pair of graceful townhouses have been transformed into a facsimile of a country inn, with a cozy fireplace-lit tea salon and 12 elegant rooms and suites featuring four-poster beds. There's a nice little restaurant on the lower level that offers room service.

Morgans

237 Madison Avenue (at 37th Street); tel: 212-686 0300; www.morganshotel. com; subway: Grand Central 42nd Street; $$$

The original brainchild of Ian Schrager and the late Steve Rubell, and, surprisingly for New York, still one of the most fashionable addresses in Manhattan; an ultra-modern enclave for hip movie stars and other millionaires. The decor's original stark, dramatic grays have been replaced by warmer tones, but there's still a minimalist ambience. Service is known to be extraordinary.

The Roger

131 Madison Avenue (at 31st Street); tel: 212-448 7000, 888-448 7788; www.the rogernewyork.com; subway: 33rd Street; $$$$

The Roger has exchanged its sleek, stark style for a warmer approach, using bold colors and natural wood. The lobby has a soaring atrium, while the bedrooms are home-away-from-home cozy, with lots of space, thick bathrobes, down comforters, and CD players. The penthouses have lovely balconies with views of the Empire State Building.

Upper West Side

Beacon Hotel

2130 Broadway (between 74th and 75th streets); tel: 212-787-1100, 800-572-4969; www.beaconhotel.com; subway: 72nd Street; $$

Newly decorated, with good-sized rooms and a convenient location, the unpretentious Beacon is a good choice, especially if you are a fan of the groups

Bemelmans Bar at the Carlyle

playing at the Beacon Theater, the musical landmark next door.

Lucerne Hotel

201 West 79th Street (at Amsterdam Avenue); tel: 212-875-1000, 800-492-8122; www.thelucernehotel.com; subway: 79th Street; $$$

A 1904 landmark building has become the gracious Lucerne, with European-inspired decor and many amenities. The hotel's Nice Matin restaurant is a favourite in the neighborhood.

Marrakech Hotel

2688 Broadway (at West 103rd Street); tel: 212-222-2954; www.marrakechhotelnyc.com; subway: 103 Street 1; $

Recently redone with colourful Moroccan decor, this definitely remains a budget spot with very small rooms, but has upgraded with amenities including all private baths, flat-screen TV, and massage shower heads. There's a café, lounge, and a Starbucks on the premises.

Milburn Hotel

242 West 76th Street; tel: 212-362-1006, 800-833-9622; www.milburnhotel.com; subway: 79th Street; $$

Located just off Broadway, with Central Park only steps away, the Milburn is well situated. The hotel's amenities are nothing out of the ordinary, yet they are clean, the price is good, and the staff are friendly. Close to a wide range of restaurants. Suites have kitchenettes, and you can stock up on groceries at nearby Fairway and Zabar's, grocery stores popular with local residents.

On The Ave Hotel

2178 Broadway (at 77th Street); tel: 212-362-1100, 800-509-7598; www.ontheave-nyc.com; subway: 79th Street; $$$

The hotel offers stylish rooms. It is within walking distance of the American Museum of Natural History and prime Upper West Side shopping.

Upper East Side

The Carlyle

35 East 76th Street (at Madison Avenue); tel: 212-744-1600, 888-767-3966; www.thecarlyle.com; subway: 77th Street 6; $$$$

Posh, reserved, and serene, the Carlyle remains a highly acclaimed luxury hotel. The appointments are exquisite, the furnishings antique, the service formal. The hotel is the home of Café Carlyle and Bemelmans Bar, two of the city's most enduring upscale evening spots.

The Franklin

164 East 87th Street (between Lexington and Third avenues); tel: 212-369-1000, 800-607-4009; www.franklinhotel.com; subway: 86th Street 4, 5, 6; $$$

This boutique hotel has upgraded and is not the bargain it once was, but look out for special rates. Despite very small rooms, the atmosphere is charming, the complimentary breakfast deli-

A light and airy suite at The Mark

cious, the beds heavenly. Guests enjoy WiFi access, nightly wine and cheese reception, 24-hour cappuccino and espresso.

Gracie Inn
502 East 81st Street (at York Avenue); tel: 212-628-1700, 800-404-2252; www.thegracieinn.com; subway: 77th Street 6; $$
On a side street in a quiet part of town near Gracie Mansion (the mayor's official residence), this place is a cross between a townhouse and a country inn. From small studios to large penthouses, rates are subject to reduction depending on the length of your stay.

The Lowell
28 East 63rd Street (at Madison Avenue); tel: 212-838-1400; 800-221-4444; www.lowellhotel.com; subway: Lexington Avenue 63rd Street; $$$$
Understated elegance is the byword at this exclusive, polished all-suite property just off chic Madison Avenue. The hotel is known for its elegant tea salon.

The Mark
Madison Avenue at 77th Street; tel: 212-744-4300, 866-744-4300; www.themarkhotel.com; subway: 77th Street; $$$$
Still fresh from a total makeover at its prestigious Upper East Side address, The Mark is a model of contemporary luxury, and boasts a celebrity chef since Jean-Georges Vongerichten came aboard in 2010. Special offers on the hotel website make it more affordable.

The Surrey
20 East 76th Street (at Madison and 5th avenues); tel: 212-288-3700, 888-419 0052; www.thesurreyhotel.com; subway: 77th Street; $$$$
This Beaux Arts gem's rooms are as elegant as any in this tony neighborhood, and the hotel is home to an impressive art collection. Grab a meal at the Café Boulud restaurant, just off the lobby; in the summer, check out the rooftop garden for a rare experience that is often exclusive to locals with penthouses.

Hotel Wales
1295 Madison Avenue (at 92nd Street); tel: 212-876-6000, 866-925-3746; www.hotelwalesnyc.com; subway: 96th Street 6; $$$
The Wales offers a great location in Carnegie Hill, near Museum Mile and Central Park. Feast on the city's best breakfast next door at Sarabeth's Kitchen, or enjoy the light one offered in the hotel's tea salon, also the setting for afternoon tea and chamber music.

Greenwich Village and the Meatpacking District
Contempo Design Suites
59 Fifth Avenue (at 13th Street); email:

reservations@contempodesignnyc.com;
www.contempodesignnyc.com; subway:
Union Square; $$$
A stylish alternative to a standard hotel,
this collection of furnished apartments
between Washington Square and Union
Square parks is available for nightly or
long-term stays.

Hotel Gansevoort
18 Ninth Avenue (at 13th Street); tel:
212-206-6700, 877-426-7386; www.hotel
gansevoort.com; subway: Eighth Avenue;
$$$$
The Meatpacking District's first luxury
hotel has a rooftop bar, swimming pool,
and breathtaking views. Bedrooms
are fashionably appointed (think neu-
tral colors and a single orchid). If your
room faces west, the Hudson River will
be on the horizon and the Meatpack-
ing action will be taking place directly
below, nonstop.

The Jane
113 Jane Street (at West Street); tel: 212-
924-6700; www.thejanenyc.com; subway:
Eighth Avenue; $
A new incarnation of a budget hotel
in a 1907 seaman's home, The Jane
has carefully kept the quirky nostalgia
while modernizing. Compact rooms
are reminiscent of seamen's bunks.
All have private baths, some offer river
views and terraces. It's a bit of a walk
to public transportation, but it is sur-
rounded by some of the city's prettiest
blocks.

The Standard Hotel
848 Washington Street (at 13th Street);
tel: 212-645 4646; www.standardhotels.
com; subway: Eighth Avenue;
$$$$
The High Line passes under the ele-
vated Standard Hotel, where rooms
are decked out with leather furniture,
glass tables, and a fully modern sheen.
In the winter, there's an ice rink. Year-
round it has one of the Meatpacking
District's most popular bars and res-
taurants, The Standard Grill.

Washington Square Hotel
103 Waverly Place (near Macdougal
Street); tel: 212-777-9515;
www.washingtonsquarehotel.com;
subway: West Fourth Street; $
A century-old hotel that offers an ideal
Village location on Washington Square
Park. The rooms are small but are nev-
ertheless nicely appointed. In a former
incarnation, this was the seedy Hotel
Earle, where Papa John Phillips of the
1960s folk group The Mamas & the
Papas wrote the folk-rock classic *Cali-
fornia Dreaming*.

Soho and Tribeca
Duane Street Hotel
130 Duane Street (near Church Street); tel:
212-964-4600, www.duanestreethotel.com;
subway: Chamber Street ; $$$
This small, sleek new contemporary
hotel offers moderate rates in a pricey
neighbourhood. An ideal bolthole for
lovers of modern boutique style.

An amazing view from the Hotel on Rivington's penthouse

Greenwich Hotel

377 Greenwich Street (near Moore Street); tel: 212-941-8900; www.thegreenwich hotel.com; subway: Franklin Street; $$$$

Robert De Niro and partners planned this exceptional luxury hotel with a residential feel. It offers a warm sitting room with fireplace and a landscaped courtyard, extra-spacious guest rooms, and an indoor pool. Rustic-elegant decor mixes Tibetan rugs, Moroccan and Italian tiles, old wood beams, and Asian antiques with paintings by De Niro's father.

Mercer Hotel

147 Mercer Street (near Prince Street); tel: 212-966-6060, 888-918-6060; www.mercerhotel.com; subway: Prince Street; $$$$

This 1890s landmark has 75 rooms with high loft ceilings, WiFi access, flat-screen televisions, and (for New York) spacious bathrooms. Andre Balazs, the owner, also owns Chateau Marmont in Los Angeles, and the clientele here is equally stylish and high profile. Facilities include a roof garden, a library bar with 24-hour service, complimentary gym access, and the highly regarded Mercer Kitchen restaurant and café.

SoHo Grand

310 W. Broadway (near Canal Street); tel: 212-965-3000; www.sohogrand.com; subway: Canal Street A, C, E; $$$$

Expect excellent service at this 15-story hotel, with industrial-chic decor and magnificent upper-floor views. Rooms have large windows. The lobby and bar are the rendezvous of choice for cool media types and rock stars.

Lower East Side

Hotel on Rivington

107 Rivington Street (near Ludlow Street); tel: 212-475-2600; www.hotelonrivington. com; subway: Delancey Street; $$$$

This sleek glass-walled hotel is bringing a dash of contemporary style to the gentrifying Lower East Side. Great Manhattan views and walking distance to many of the most popular districts.

Lower Manhattan

Best Western Seaport Inn

33 Peck Slip (at Front Street); tel: 212-766-6600, 800-HOTEL-NY; www.bestwestern. com; subway: Fulton Street 2, 3; $$

This converted 19th-century warehouse has 72 rooms with Federal-style furnishings. Some rooms have views of the Brooklyn Bridge.

Holiday Inn Express Wall Street

126 Water Street (at Pine Street); tel: 212-747-9222, 888-HOLIDAY; www.holidayinn.com; subway: Wall Street 2, 3; $$

Business and pleasure meet here, with high-speed internet and work stations in every room as well as homey touches.

Hip design at Blue Fin

RESTAURANTS

In a city with more than 20,000 restaurants, New Yorkers dine out a lot. With restaurants just steps from their doors there is no reason for them not to enjoy the best the city has to offer, and visitors should do the same. You'll find some of the best restaurants in the country in New York, and some are quite expensive. But you won't have to take out a second mortgage on your home to eat well in this city – even in Manhattan. The variety of restaurants and eating options is unsurpassed. You can enjoy Indian dosas from a street vendor, dine at the newest celebrity chef's restaurant, or simply enjoy a really great meal at a favorite neighborhood spot.

Midtown

21

21 W. 52nd Street (at 5th and 6th avenues); tel: 212-582 7200; www.21club.com; Tue–Fri L and D, Mon and Sat D; subway: Fifth Avenue 53rd Street; $$$$

This ex-speakeasy will never be out of style with Manhattan's movers and shakers. Miniature jockeys line the

> Price guide for a three-course dinner for one:
> $$$$ = over $70
> $$$ = $50–70
> $$ = $25–50
> $ = under $25

exterior, while other corporate toys hang from the ceiling. A plaque over Table 30 reads 'Bogie's Corner.' Sip his favorite tipple, Ramos gin fizz, and order the chicken hash.

Becco

355 West 46th Street (between Eighth and Ninth avenues); tel: 212-397-7597; http://becco-nyc.com; daily L and D; subway: 49th Street N, R, W; $$

Lidia Bastianich's restaurant row mainstay offers three daily pasta preparations for less than $25 and bottles of wine for under $30. One of the city's great deals.

Blue Fin

W Times Square Hotel, 1567 Broadway (between 46th and 47th streets); tel: 212-918-1400; www.bluefinnyc.com; daily B, L, and D; subway: 49th Street N, R, W; $$$

It's easy to be swept away by this seafood restaurant's over-the-top decor; in the street-level bar only a glass wall separates diners from the hubbub of Times Square, and Austin Powers would feel at home in the retro dining room. The sushi is sublime, and 'cooked' dishes such as sesame-crusted tuna and pan-roasted bass are a close second.

Brasserie Ruhlmann

45 Rockefeller Plaza (between Fifth and Sixth avenues); tel: 212-974-2020;

Elegance at Four Seasons   *Four Seasons' bar*

www.brasserieruhlmann.com; Mon–Sat L
and D, Sun Br; subway: 47–50 Streets –
Rockefeller Center; $$$

A bit of 1920s Paris in Rockefeller
Center. This inviting café was named
for Art Deco designer Emile-Jacques
Ruhlmann and pays homage with Deco
decor. Chef Laurent Tourondel gets top
marks for his bistro offerings. The shady
patio invites lingering.

Bryant Park Grill

25 West 40th Street (at Sixth Avenue); tel:
212-840-6500; www.arkrestaurants.com/
bryant_park; daily L and D; subway: Fifth
Avenue 7; $$$

A wall of glass and a generous terrace
make the most of the park's leafy sur-
roundings. The food almost lives up to
the setting, with a menu of grilled and
roasted fish and meats.

DB Bistro Moderne

55 West 44th Street (near Sixth Avenue);
tel: 212-391-2400; www.dbbistro.com;
daily B, L and D; subway: 47–50 Streets –
Rockefeller Center; $$$$

So modern that its menu is organized
by ingredients, chef Daniel Boulud's
bistro is awash with Art Deco glitz and
well-heeled publishing types and trendy
tourists. The foie gras-and-truffle burger
is typical of the kitchen's culinary sur-
prises.

Four Seasons

99 East 52nd Street (between Lexington
and Park avenues); tel: 212-754 9494;
www.fourseasonsrestaurant.com; Mon–Fri
L and D, Sat D only; subway: Lexington
Avenue/51st Street; $$$$

Since it opened nearly 50 years ago, the
Four Seasons in the landmark Seagram
Building has had a clientele to rival any
Who's Who listing. The decor is price-
less and the seasonal classics served
are impeccable.

La Bonne Soupe

48 West 55th Street (between Fifth
and Sixth avenues); tel: 212-586-7650;
http://labonnesoupe.com; daily L and D;
subway: N, R, or F to 57th Street; $–$$

When cash is low, head for this old-time
French bistro, a standby since 1973
for crepes, quiche, fondues, and great
onion soup as well as *steak frites* and
poulet. Reserve ahead or be prepared
to stand in line.

La Grenouille

3 East 52nd Street (between Fifth and
Madison avenues); tel: 212-752 1495;
http://la-grenouille.com; Tue–Sat L and D;
subway: Fifth Avenue/53rd Street; $$$$

One of the last of the great French eater-
ies in Midtown, where a quenelle is still
a quenelle and the flowers have rarely
been more beautiful. A classic.

Michael Jordan's The SteakHouse NYC

Grand Central Terminal (42nd Street
and Park Avenue); tel: 212-655-2300;
www.michaeljordansnyc.com; daily L and D;
subway: Grand Central Terminal; $$$

High-end dining at Jean-Georges

The basketball star's steakhouse offers slabs of dry-aged beef on a balcony overlooking Grand Central Terminal's magnificent concourse.

Oceana

120 W. 49th Street (at 6th and 7th avenues); tel: 212-759 5941; http://oceanarestaurant.com; Mon–Fri L and D, Sat–Sun D; subway: 47–50 Streets – Rockefeller Center; $$$$

Spectacular seafood and one of the city's best raw bars served in the ground floor of the McGraw Hill Building. If tables aren't available, the 50ft (15-meter) marble bar is gorgeous and a good alternative.

Smith & Wollensky

797 Third Avenue (49th Street); tel: 212-753-1530; www.smithandwollenskynyc.com; daily L and D; subway: 51st Street 6; $$$

This New York institution is usually packed with stockbrokers and Midtown executives, who come for the great steaks, extensive American wine list, and clubby, masculine atmosphere. The adjacent Wollensky's Grill is more casual and a bit less expensive.

Trattoria Dell'Arte

900 Seventh Avenue (at 56th Street); tel: 212-245-9800; www.trattoriadellarte.com; daily L and D; subway: 57th Street/Seventh Avenue; $$$

The fabulous antipasto bar doubles as a main course at this popular trattoria near Carnegie Hall. The seafood, pasta, and gourmet pizza are good choices, too.

Via Brasil

34 West 46th Street (between Fifth and Sixth Avenues); tel: 212-997-1158; www.viabrasilrestaurant.com; daily L and D; subway: 47–50 Streets – Rockefeller Center; $$

On the street known as 'Little Brazil,' this is a great place to try authentic specialties including big portions of beef *feijoada*, a stew that is the Brazilian national dish. There are chicken and fish dishes, too, if you don't favour red meat.

Upper West Side

Dizzy's Club Coca-Cola

33 West 60th Street (near Broadway); tel: 212-258-9595; http://jalc.org/dizzys; daily D; subway: 59th Street Columbus Circle; $$

The music and menu are red hot at Jazz at Lincoln Center's supper club, which dishes out Latin and Creole cuisine with a side of live jazz.

Dovetail

103 W. 77th Street (at Columbus Aveneu); tel: 212-362 3800; http://dovetailnyc.com; Mon–Fri D, Sat–Sun Br and D; subway: 79th Street; $$$$

Heralded as the best restaurant to hit the Upper West Side in ages, this instant classic, serving New American cuisine, can be found behind the American Museum of Natural History.

Jean-Georges

Trump International Hotel, 1 Central Park West; tel: 212-299-3900; Mon–Sat L and D, Sun Br; subway: 59th Street Columbus Circle; $$$

A gourmet dessert at Daniel   *Daniel's dining room*

The skyscraper on chaotic Columbus Circle is an unlikely location for one of the city's most sophisticated and relaxing retreats. Chef Jean-Georges Vongerichten delights diners with creative versions of French classics. The bill can soar as high as the building, but the *prix-fixe* lunch at the adjoining Nougatine brings these gastronomic heights within reach. Book ahead.

Kefi

505 Columbus Avenue (between 84th and 85th streets); tel: 212-873-0200; http://kefi restaurant.com; Mon–Fri L and D, Sat–Sun Br and D; subway: 86th Street B, C; $$

One of the finest Greek restaurants in the city, where the crowd is always lively and the food is simultaneously comforting, traditional, and innovative.

Harlem

Amy Ruth's

113 West 116th Street (between Lenox and Seventh avenues); tel: 212-280-8779; www.amyruthsharlem.com; Tue–Sun B, L, and D, Mon L and D; subway: 116th Street; $

This restaurant attracts celebrities from the worlds of politics, sports, and entertainment, but the big pull is the classic Southern food.

Upper East Side

Beyoglu

1431 Third Avenue (at 81st Street), 2nd floor; tel: 212-650-0850; daily L and D; subway: 77th Street 6; $$

Middle Eastern flavors burst from dishes such as yogurt rice soup, lamb kebab, hummus, and sauteed eggplant at this meze restaurant named after an Istanbul neighborhood. The portions are ideal for sharing, so come with a group and explore the whole menu.

Daniel

60 East 65th Street (near Park Avenue); tel: 212-288-0033; http://danielnyc.com; Mon–Sat D; subway: Lexington Avenue/63rd Street; $$$$

Master chef Daniel Boulud presides over this expensive food kingdom, but gourmets will gladly spend for the unique quality and service he delivers. The cuisine is mostly French with a few unexpected (but not gimmicky) twists, and the service is impeccable.

L'Absinthe

227 East 67th Street (between Second and Third avenues); tel: 212-794-4950; http://labsinthe.com; Mon–Sat L and D, Sun Br and D; subway: 68th Street/Hunter College; $$$

The etched mirrors, polished brass, and French waiters in white aprons are as authentic as the classic brasserie fare.

The Loeb Boathouse

Park Drive North; tel: 212-517-2233; www.thecentralparkboathouse.com; Apr–Nov daily L and D, Sat–Sun Br; subway: 77th Street 6; $$$$

A great lakefront setting either in the airy, glass-fronted dining room or on the waterside terrace. Seafood is a spe-

cialty here, along with the pan-seared rack of lamb.

Spigolo

1561 Second Avenue (at 81st Street); tel: 212-744-1100; www.spigolonyc.com; Mon–Fri D, Sat–Sun Br and D; subway: 77th Street; $$$

A husband-wife team trained at Union Square Café have created a tiny gem widely recognized for exceptional Italian fare. Reserve well in advance.

Chelsea to Gramercy Park

Cookshop

156 Tenth Avenue (at 20th Street); tel: 212-924-4440; Mon–Fri B, L and D; Sat–Sun Br and D; www.cookshopny.com; subway: 23rd Street; $$

Support from local farmers means the freshest ingredients at this unpretentious Chelsea spot with good American food. Weekend brunches are wildly popular.

Friend of a Farmer

77 Irving Place (between 18th and 19th streets); tel: 212-477-2188; http://friendofa farmerny.com; Mon–Fri B, L, and D, Sat–Sun Br and D; subway: Union Square; $$

It feels like a Vermont inn at this cozy restaurant serving hearty portions of American fare. Great for families.

Gramercy Tavern

42 East 20th Street (between Broadway and Park Avenue); tel: 212-477-0777; www.gramercytavern.com; Mon–Fri L and D, Sat–Sun D; subway: Union Square; $$$$

The Gramercy's New American cuisine is artfully prepared, and the handsome dining room has a homey feeling. Be sure to leave room for the chocolate bread pudding.

Half King

505 West 23rd Street (at Tenth Avenue); tel: 212-462-4300; www.thehalfking. com; Mon–Fri L and D, Sat–Sun Br and D; subway: 23rd Street C, E; $

Just the sort of easygoing place that Chelsea could use more of. The bar and dining room serve as a gallery for artists and photojournalists, and the garden is a snug retreat. The fish and chips, shepherd's pie, burgers, and other pub fare are fairly priced.

Novità

102 East 22nd Street (between Park and Lexington avenues); tel: 212-677-2222; www.novitanyc.com; Mon–Fri L and D, Sat–Sun D; subway: 23rd Street 6; $$$

This northern Italian restaurant remains an undiscovered gem. Expect delicious, freshly prepared dishes, gracious service, and reasonable prices.

Union Square Café

21 East 16th Street (between Fifth Avenue and Union Square); tel: 212-243-4020; http://unionsquarecafe.com; daily L and D; subway: Union Square; $$$$

A winning formula of top-flight food and service makes this a favorite of residents and tourists alike. The atmosphere is

The Loeb Boathouse's special location

casual, but in a studied way. The chefs make full use of local ingredients sold by farmers at Union Square's Greenmarket to create a menu of mostly American fare, with a distinctly Italian accent.

Greenwich Village and the Meatpacking District

AOC

314 Bleecker Street (at Grove Street); tel: 212-675 9463; www.aocnyc.com; daily B, L, and D; subway: Christopher Street Sheridan Square; $$

The dishes are served here as simply and perfectly as in a Paris bistro. Unlike other hurried New York spots, here *le savoir-vivre* reigns, and you can linger and talk all night if no one needs your table. There's a little garden patio for summer, too.

Blue Hill

75 Washington Place (between Sixth Avenue and Washington Square West); tel: 212-539-1776; www.bluehillfarm.com; daily D; subway: West 4th Street; $$$$

A mellow, sophisticated spot that gets rave reviews for beautifully conceived American dishes made with fresh ingredients from the Blue Hill family farm.

CamaJe

85 Macdougal Street (between Bleecker and Houston streets); tel: 212-673-8184; http://camaje.com; daily L and D; subway: West Fourth Street; $$

Chef Abigail Hitchcock prepares top-notch French bistro dishes with imagination and heart. The casual atmosphere and reasonable prices make this a real find.

Da Silvano

260 Sixth Avenue (between Bleecker and Houston streets); tel: 212-982-2343; http://dasilvano.com; daily L and D; subway: Houston Street; $$$

Simple, flavorful Tuscan cuisine attracts a loyal following, including quite a few celebrities. A less expensive option is next door at Bar Pitti, run by the same folks, with similar Tuscan tastes.

Del Posto

85 Tenth Avenue (between 15th and 16th streets); tel: 212-497-8090; www.delposto.com; Mon–Fri L and D, Sat–Sun D; subway: 14th Street; $$$

Mario Batali's most ambitious showplace on the edge of the Meatpacking District lives up to its palazzo feel, with Italian food that reviewers have called 'heavenly.' Despite the formal setting, the staff is friendly and the piano music relaxing. The Italian wine list is enormous.

Fatty Crab

643 Hudson Street (between Horatio and Gansevoort); tel: 212-352-3592; www.fattycrab.com; daily L and D, Sat–Sun Br; subway: Eighth Avenue; $$-$$$

This isn't authentic Asian food, but the fare at this cubby hole of a restaurant combines Asian flavors in unique and inventive ways. Try the signature crab, the watermelon pickle and crispy pork, the sliders and the duck.

Ever-trendy Pastis

Mexicana Mama

525 Hudson Street (between Charles and West 10th streets); tel: 212-924-4119; Tue–Sun L and D; subway: Christopher Street/Sheridan Square; $$

This tiny Mexican spot is worth the wait to get in. The menu is limited, but the boldly flavored dishes are a far cry from average Tex-Mex fare. A taco here is a culinary masterpiece. Cash only.

Pastis

9 Ninth Avenue (at Little West 12th Street); tel: 212-929-4844; www.pastisny.com; Mon–Fri B, L and D, Sat–Sun Br and D; subway: Eighth Avenue; $$$

Long one of the most popular eateries in the Meatpacking District, the air around Pastis buzzes with beautiful people, limos, and taxis. In spite of this, it retains the feel of an old-fashioned brasserie (with furnishings brought over from Europe).

Pearl Oyster Bar

18 Cornelia Street (between Bleecker and West Fourth streets); tel: 212-691-8211; www.pearloysterbar.com; Mon–Fri L and D, Sat D; subway: West Fourth Street; $$

This raw bar is tucked into a side street populated by other small restaurants. Chowder is served, in addition to what some call 'perfection on the half-shell.'

Spice Market

403 West 13th Street (at Ninth Avenue); tel: 212-675-2322; www.spicemarketnewyork.com; daily L and D; subway: 14th Street/Eighth Avenue; $$

Celebrity chef Jean-Georges Vongerichten oversees a spicy menu inspired by Asian street fare at this stylish, two-floor warehouse space.

The Spotted Pig

314 West 11th Street (at Greenwich Street); tel: 212-620-0393; http://thespottedpig.com; daily L and D; subway: Christopher Street; $$

Thanks to chef April Bloomfield, this tiny, casual restaurant elevates pub food to gourmet status. Sit on plump cushions at small tables or perch on a stool and dig into chicken liver parfait, squid and mussel salad, or slow-braised beef shin with risotto. For a calmer scene, visit at lunch.

East Village, Little Italy, and Lower East Side

Caracas Arepa Bar

93 ½ E. 7th Street (at 1st Avenue and Avenue A); tel: 212-228 5062; www.caracasarepabar.com; daily L and D; subway: Astor Place; $ ¢

Locals flock to this casual Venezuelan restaurant for: warm cornmeal pancakes topped with savory meat and vegetable options, and served with hot sauce.

Indochine

430 Lafayette Street (at Astor Place and 4th Street); tel: 212-505 5111; www.indochinenyc.com; daily D; subway: Astor Place; $$$

Dining in Little Italy

Trendy, tropical decor, French-Vietnamese food, still sexy after all these years. It's located across from the Public Theater, and offers a decently priced pre-theater deal.

Momofuku Noodle Bar

171 First Avenue (between 10th and 11th streets); tel: 212-777-7773; http://momofuku.com; daily L and D; subway: First Avenue; $$

The original outpost of the Momofuku empire, a hip place to get a bowl of ramen, some peerless pork buns, and a Korean-style fried chicken dinner for four. Also check out Momofuku Saam Bar, Ko, and Milk Bar, all in the neighborhood.

Puglia

189 Hester Street (at Mulberry Street); tel: 212-966-6006; www.pugliaofnyc.com; daily L and D; subway: Canal Street J, N, Q, R, 6; $$

The Little Italy of old has persisted here since 1919. Things get 'pretty crazy' at night, according to the manager Joey, but group tables, a singer called 'The Fat Lady,' plus lots of red sauce and red wine make it a party every night.

WD~50

50 Clinton Street (at Rivington and Stanton); tel: 212-477 2900; http://wd-50.com; daily D; subway: Essex Street; $$$$

WD stands for Wally Dufresne, who presides over a brilliant American-eclectic menu and is one of the originators and innovators of the molecular gastronomy movement.

Soho

Balthazar

80 Spring Street (near Crosby Street); tel: 212-965-1414; www.balthazarny.com; daily B and D, Mon–Fri L, Sat–Sun Br; subway: Spring Street; $$$

Parisian-style brasserie serving traditional bistro fare from breakfast until late. This spot is so popular, it's now hard to imagine Soho without it.

Blue Ribbon

97 Sullivan Street (at Spring Street); tel: 212-274-0404; www.blueribbonrestaurants.com; daily D; subway: Spring Street C, E; $$$

Popular for over 20 years, this Soho dining room and nightspot boasts an excellent raw bar and robust American classics. It's open late for bar crawlers, night owls and chefs coming off their shifts.

Bread

20 Spring Street (near Elizabeth Street); tel: 212-334-1015; daily L and D; subway: Spring Street 6; $

This tiny café and wine bar celebrates bread and all that can go between it. Hot panini are filled with everything from pesto chicken, avocado, and goat's cheese to shiitake mushrooms, fresh sardines, and tomatoes. There are salads and pastas as well.

Tribeca hotspot Odeon

Corton

239 W. Broadway (at White and North Main streets); tel: 212-219 2777; www.cortonnyc.com; Tue–Sat D; subway: Canal Street; $$$$

Some of the city's most refined French cuisine in a decidedly modern dining room. Justly celebrated as one of the best new restaurants. Closed in July.

Jane

100 West Houston Street (near Thompson Street); tel: 212-254-7000; http://jane restaurant.com; Mon–Sat L and D, Sun Br and D; subway: Houston Street or Spring Street; $$

There's nothing plain about this Jane, where creative American dishes such as honey-braised pork and grilled sirloin are crafted from fresh, locally grown ingredients. Be sure to leave room for dessert.

Tribeca

Bouley

163 Duane Street (at West Broadway); tel: 212-964-2525; www.davidbouley.com; daily L and D; subway: Chambers Street 1, 2, 3; $$$$

Fans claim that experiencing David Bouley's 'new French' food transcends price. Perhaps a better way to put it is that eating at this elegantly hip restaurant is, at its best, a transcendent culinary experience...if you can afford it.

Bubby's

120 Hudson Street (at North Moore Street); tel: 212-219-0666; www.bubbys.com; daily

B, L, and D; subway: Franklin Street; $

This place feels like a farmhouse kitchen transplanted into the city. Every order comes with a basket of biscuits, and the menu boasts 'food like Mom would make if she only knew how.' Open 24 hours, except for Tuesdays from midnight–7am.

Nobu

105 Hudson Street (between Franklin and North Moore streets); tel: 212-219-0500; www.noburestaurants.com; Mon–Fri L and D, Sat D; subway: Franklin Street; $$$$

Celebrity-spotting is a favorite pastime at this Tribeca hotspot, justly acclaimed for chef Nobu Matsuhisa's Japanese-Peruvian cuisine. It is virtually impossible to book a table, but Nobu Next Door (no reservations accepted) is a good second choice.

Odeon

145 W. Broadway (at Duane and Thomas streets); tel: 212-233-0507; theodeon restaurant.com; Mon–Fri L and D Sat–Sun Br and D; subway: Franklin Street; $$$

One of the first Tribeca hotspots, this Art Deco brasserie has been a mainstay ever since Warhol and Basquiat used to drop by. It's open from 10am on weekends (11.30 weekdays) for dining; enjoy fewer crowds earlier in the day.

Tribeca Grill

375 Greenwich Street (at Crosby Street); tel: 212-941-3900; www.myriad restaurantgroup.com; Mon–Fri and Sun L

Enjoy superb sushi at Nobu

and D, Sat D only; subway: Franklin Street; $$$

Co-owned by actor Robert De Niro and chef Drew Nieporent, customers flock here in the hope of seeing celebs from the Tribeca Film Center talking 'back story' and making deals.

Lower Manhattan

Bridge Café

279 Water Street, at Dover Street; tel: 212-227-3344; http://bridgecafenyc.com; daily L and D; subway: Fulton Street 2, 3; $$

Seafood, steaks, whiskey and beer in the city's oldest tavern (and one time brothel), which was fully renovated after Hurricane Sandy. The building dates back to 1794, nearly 90 years before the Brooklyn Bridge was constructed

Delmonico's

56 Beaver Street (at William Street); tel: 212-509-1144; www.delmonicos restaurantgroup.com; Mon–Fri L and D, Sat D; subway: Wall Street 2, 3; $$$$

Wall Street deal-makers congregate at this clubby, chummy, old-time steakhouse. Beef is the specialty, of course, but the lobster, oysters Rockefeller, and other seafood dishes are quite good, too.

Gigino at Wagner Park

20 Battery Place (at West Street); tel: 212-528-2228; www.gigino-wagnerpark.com; daily L and D; subway: Bowling Green; $$

With sunset views of the Statue of Liberty, this moderately priced Italian could easily pander to tourists, but the food is high-quality and creative. When the weather is fine, the terrace is irresistible.

Harry's Café

1 Hanover Square (at Pearl and Stone streets); tel: 212-785 9200; www.harrysnyc.com; Mon–Sat L and D; subway: Wall Street 2, 3; $$

Folks refused to accept that the original Harry's closed, so the owners reopened it, offering great steaks and seafood.

Brooklyn

Applewood

501 11th Street; tel: 718-788-1810; www.applewoodny.com; Mon–Fri D, Sat Br and D, Sun Br; subway: Seventh Avenue; $$$

With a lovely leafy terrace, this unpretentious restaurant serves outstanding food, with the emphasis on seasonal, ethically sourced, local ingredients. It's an excellent choice for a meal (from 5pm) at the end of a day in Brooklyn, or Sunday brunch.

The Bronx

Roberto's

632 Crescent Avenue (at 186th Street); tel: 718-733-9503; www.roberto089.com; Mon–Sat L and D; train: Fordham; $$

Roberto will pop out of the kitchen in his whites to meet and greet, while his floury-handed mama may say hello in between preparing batches of pasta. A true slice of Italian life. When it's time to leave, catch a cab to Fordham Road station; you should take extra care in this neighborhood.

Queues at BB King's Blues Club & Grill

NIGHTLIFE

The opportunities for entertainment and nightlife in New York could provide different diversions 365 days a year. Additionally, note that summer brings free Shakespeare, opera, and popular music concerts to Central Park. There is also free music and outdoor movies in many city parks.

Theater

Broadway
New York's Theater District is home to 40 active theaters, most on the side streets off Broadway, spanning Sixth to Eighth avenues between 41st and 53rd streets. For a list of current shows and theaters, see www.ilovenytheater.com.

Lincoln Center Theater
150 West 65th Street between Broadway and Amsterdam Avenue; tel: 212-239-6200; www.lct.org
The 1080-seat Vivian Beaumont and the 299-seat Newhouse, Lincoln Center stage both large-scale and intimate musical and dramatic plays.

Manhattan Theatre Club
Samuel Friedman Theater, 261 West 47th Street, tel: 212-239-6200; Stage 1, New York City Center, 131 West 55th Street; tel: 212-581-1212; www.manhattan theatreclub.org
Founded in 1970, this company produces many notable plays, including American premieres of works by playwrights such as Alan Ayckbourn.

Public Theater
425 Lafayette Street (between East 4th Street and Astor Place); tel: 212-539-8500; www.publictheater.org
Founded as the Shakespeare Workshop and still sponsors of free Shakespeare in the Park, the Public has grown into a showcase for the new and experimental. *Hair* and *A Chorus Line* were born here.

Roundabout Theatre Company
Tel: 212-719-1300; www.roundabout theatre.org
The city's largest repertory company with 40,000 subscribers, four theaters, and countless awards, the Roundabout was founded in 1965 to revive classics. It later expanded to include new works.

Live music

BB King's Blues Club & Grill
237 West 42nd Street; tel: 212-997 4144; www.bbkingblues.com
In the heart of Times Square, the legendary bluesman's New York venture (there are others around the country, including Memphis) packs them in for the best of the biggest names in R&B. This can include the King himself, stroking the only thing that's never let him down – his guitar, Lucille.

Many special events are held at Carnegie Hall

The Bitter End

147 Bleecker Street, between Thompson and Laguardia; tel: 212-673 7030; www.bitterend.com

A Greenwich Village landmark, the Bitter End books an eclectic mishmash of folk, folk rock, soft rock, blues, some comedy and cabaret... whatever. A classic example of eternal bohemianism, it's popular with tourists and can be mobbed on weekends.

Bowery Ballroom

6 Delancey Street (between Bowery and Christie streets); tel: 212-533-2111; www.boweryballroom.com

The 'in' spot to hear the best bands in concert, including top indie-rock bands.

Brooklyn Academy of Museum

30 Lafayette Avenue, Brooklyn; tel: 718-636-4100; www.bam.org

Best known as BAM, the city's oldest performing arts center is also the most progressive, offering avant-garde companies in dance, music, opera, and theater. Easy to reach by subway or the BAMbus serving Manhattan.

Carnegie Hall

57th Street (at Seventh Avenue); tel: 212-247-7800; www.carnegiehall.org

Famed for its acoustics since its opening in 1891, this landmark concert hall seating 2,800 presents the world's top musicians and orchestras, from classical to jazz.

Lincoln Center

Broadway (between 63rd and 65th streets); schedules and tickets for all except Metropolitan Opera, tel: 212-721-6500; opera tickets, tel: 212-362-6000; www.lincoln center.org

The city's cultural hub is home to the Metropolitan Opera House; the New York City Ballet at the David Koch Theater; the New York Philharmonic Orchestra at Avery Fisher Hall; the Chamber Music Society of Lincoln Center; and the Juilliard School of Music.

New York City Center

West 55th Street (between Sixth and Seventh avenues); tel: 212-581-1212; www.nycitycenter.org

This 1923 building was Manhattan's first performing arts center, and the 2,730-seat auditorium hosts dance companies like Paul Taylor and Alvin Ailey, as well as the much-loved Encores series, revivals of vintage musicals.

Webster Hall

125 East 11th Street; tel: 212-353 1600; www.websterhall.com

Discount passes can be had by booking online for this large, always-jam-packed East Village club which attracts a young crowd. Open Wednesdays to Saturdays from 10pm, it offers all-night dance sessions for fans of everything from rock, reggae, and R&B to house, techno, and who knows; theme nights range from 'runway parties' to 1960s psychedelia. Recently, it has been welcoming big-

Village Vanguard

name rock and rap acts in its Grand Ballroom.

Jazz venues

Blue Note

131 West 3rd Street; tel: 212-475 8592; www.bluenote.net

The West Village is home to the most famous jazz clubs in the world, and first and foremost is the Blue Note, packed virtually every night for years. The reason is simple: the club presents the very best of mainstream jazz and blues, from time-honored greats to more contemporary acts. The line-up has featured such luminaries as the Modern Jazz Quartet, Etta James, Joe Williams, Betty Carter, the Count Basie Orchestra... the list goes on and on. For diehard fans, there's a late-night session that jams until 4am, after the last set.

Iridium

1650 Broadway (at 51st Street); tel: 212-582 2121

Relocated from the Upper West Side, this club/restaurant has presented some of jazz's most gifted denizens. Definitely worth checking out, especially Monday nights, when late guitar legend Les Paul's backing band is often holding court and hosting notable musicians like Marshall Crenshaw and Graham Parker.

Jazz at Lincoln Center

23 West 60th Street, Time Warner Center; tel: 212-258-9800; www.jalc.org

This showcase for jazz high atop the Time Warner Center, opened in 2004, includes the 1,233-seat Rose Theater for concerts and the Jazz Hall of Fame. The Allen Room for cabaret and Dizzy's Club Coca-Cola, a jazz club, feature walls of glass framing city lights.

Smoke

2751 Broadway (between 105th and 106th streets); tel: 212-864 6662; http://smoke jazz.com

Latin jazz, jazz, blues, and soul vocalists at this Uptown haunt; no cover charge for most late-night shows.

Village Vanguard

178 Seventh Ave South; tel: 212-255 4037; www.villagevanguard.com

Born over 70 years ago in a Greenwich Village basement, this flagship club cut its teeth helping to launch talents like Miles Davis and John Coltrane. In its adulthood, it hardly keeps up with the 'vanguard' anymore, but presents the greats and near-greats of what is now the mainstream. It's also a chance to catch acts that rarely tour. The VV is a terrific evening out, but an extremely popular one – call well in advance or book online to avoid disappointment.

Nightclubs

Bemelmans Bar

The Carlyle, 35 East 76th Street and Madison Avenue; tel: 212-744-1600; www.thecarlyle.com

Drinking in the West Village

Slam poetry at Nuyorican Poets Café

Charming Bemelmans murals are the backdrop at this upscale gem offering the best in jazz combos, piano, and song.

Cielo

18 West Little 12th Street; tel: 212-645-5700; www.cieloclub.com

Meat Packing District clubs come and go, but Cielo seems to stay on top, with the best DJs and loyal fans packing the sunken dance floor.

Joe's Pub

425 Lafayette Street, Public Theater; tel: 212-539-8778; www.joespub.com

Cabaret, jazz, rock, poetry – eclectic shows are always excellent here, the atmosphere is intimate, and you can order drinks and dinner to enjoy during the show.

Pacha

618 West 46th Street (between Eleventh and Twelfth avenues); tel: 212-209-7500; www.pachanyc.com

Glamour abounds at this far west side club with four levels, state-of-the-art lighting and top spinners. A happening scene.

SOB's

200 Varick Street (between Hudson Street and Sixth Avenue); tel: 212-243-4940; www.sobs.com

Sounds of Brazil are only the start. Reggae to blues or hip hop might be on at this lively club, which also offers dinner and dancing.

Comedy and cabaret

Don't Tell Mama

343 West 46th Street; www.donttellmama nyc.com, tel: 212-757 0788.

A merry spot, long-favored by a theatrical crowd. In the front there's a piano bar; the back room is non-stop cabaret, with comedians and torch singers. Leave inhibitions behind, and bring cash (no credit cards accepted for cover and drink minimum).

The Metropolitan Room

34 West 22nd Street; tel: 212-206 0440; www.metropolitanroom.com,

Sophisticated classic cabaret performers, as well as talented newcomers. An elegant yet surprisingly affordable New York night out that has a reasonable cover charge along with the usual two-drink minimum.

Nuyorican Poets Café

236 East 3rd Street (between Avenues B and C); tel: 212-780 9386; www.nuyorican.org

From poetry slams and hip-hop to multimedia, comedy, and music, at a cutting-edge East Village landmark.

Upright Citizens Brigade Theater

207 West 26th Street; tel: 212-366 9176; www.ucbtheatre.com

Improv comedy at its most bizarre and inventive. This is where television stars like Amy Poehler and many cast members of *Saturday Night Live* got their start – they still take the stage from time to time.

On Fifth Avenue

A–Z

A

Airports and arrivals

New York's major international airports are John F. Kennedy and Liberty International in nearby New Jersey. Allow an hour's driving time for each, more during rush hours. LaGuardia, serving domestic flights only, is a 30-minute drive.

AirTrain is a subway-to-rail connection between JFK and the city (tel: 877-535-2478; www.airtrainjfk.com), or there are regular trains from Penn Station to Newark Airport (tel: 888-EWR-INFO; www.airtrainnewark.com). NYC Airporter (tel: 855-269-2247; www.nycairporter.com) operates buses to and from LaGuardia and JFK from the Port Authority Bus Terminal, Penn Station, Grand Central Terminal, and some Midtown hotels. Olympia Trails (tel: 877-8-NEWARK; www.CoachUSA.com/Olympia) runs express buses between Newark Airport and the Port Authority Bus Terminal, Penn Station, and Grand Central Terminal.

Door-to-door minibus service between Manhattan and all airports is provided by Super Shuttle (tel: 800-258-3826; www.supershuttle.com) and AirLink (tel: 212-812-9000; www.goairlinkshuttle.com). Prices are attractive, but allow an extra two hours for additional passenger pickups on the way.

Taxis to Midtown run $30-35 from LaGuardia, fixed price $52 from JFK, about $55 from Newark, plus tolls. Many travelers use private limo services such as Carmel (tel: 212-666-6666; www.carmellimo.com), with rates only slightly more than taxicabs.

C

Children

Preparation – and lots of patience – are the keys to a successful trip with children. In some respects, New York is the perfect family destination because there are so many activities that both adults and children will enjoy: a Broadway show, for example, or a trip to the Central Park Zoo. For kids who aren't accustomed to big-city life, even mundane experiences will be an adventure. You may be smitten by the city's art and culture, but what your kids may remember most is riding the subway, a playground or bike ride through Central Park, or buying hot dogs from a street vendor.

Climate and clothes

New York City has four distinct seasons (see page 9). Average annual rainfall is 44in (112cm); raincoats and umbrellas are a good idea year-round.

Dress tends to be casual, but it is advisable to ask about smarter dress for restaurants, nightclubs, etc.

Harlem streets *A classic New York building in Chinatown*

Crime and safety

Despite its recent reputation as a 'caring, sharing New York,' parts of the city can hold hazards, and visitors should not be lulled into a false sense of security. Adopt the typical New Yorker's guise of looking street-smart and aware at all times and avoid ostentatious displays of jewelry or wealth that invite muggers. Excursions into deserted areas at night (such as Central Park or Battery Park) are equally unwise. Lock your hotel door even when you are inside, and travel to neighborhoods like Harlem in a group. Although Times Square has thrown off its seedy reputation, the crowded streets around this area attract pickpockets, so keep wallets in a secure place.

Although the subways are much safer than they were, people traveling alone late at night should stay on alert. Once through the turnstile, stay within sight of the ticket booth and try to get on a car where there are other people.

Customs regulations

For information on US Customs regulations, go to www.cbp.gov.

Disabled travelers

All city buses and a few major subway stops are accessible, as are most restaurants. Disabled travelers can obtain information about rights and special facilities from the Mayor's Office for People with Disabilities (tel: 212-788-2830; www.nyc.gov/mopd).

Driving in New York

Driving is the least efficient way to get around. Drivers are aggressive, traffic is frequently snarled, street parking is scant (and tickets are punitive), and commercial parking is extremely expensive.

If a car is needed, rentals are available at airports and all over the city. You must be at least 21 to rent a car, have a valid driver's license, and a major credit card. Be sure you are insured for both collision and personal liability.

Dogs

If you're traveling with a dog, keep in mind that it must be leashed in public places, and droppings must be cleaned up and disposed of properly. Scoopers are sold at pet shops and hardware stores, but many dog owners find it easier to use a plastic bag.

Drinking age

The legal drinking age in New York is 21. Be prepared to show picture identification before purchasing alcohol or entering a bar. Some nightclubs admit under-21 patrons but card everyone who attempts to buy a drink.

Electricity

Standard American electric current is 110 volts. An adapter is necessary for

European appliances, which run on 220–240 volts.

Embassies and consulates

Australia Mission to the UN: 150 East 42nd Street; tel: 212-351-6600.
British Consulate-General: 845 Third Avenue; tel: 212-745-0200.
Canadian Consulate-General: 1251 Sixth Avenue; tel: 212-596-1628.
Consulate General of Ireland: 345 Park Avenue; tel: 212-319-2555.
New Zealand Mission to the UN: 600 Third Avenue; tel: 212-826-1960.
Consulate of South Africa: 333 East 38th Street; tel: 212-213-4880.

Emergency numbers

Police, fire, ambulance: tel: 911.
Referral service: tel: 311.
Dental emergency: tel: 212-486-9458.
Health emergency: tel: 212-737-1212.
Report Sex Crimes: tel: 212-227-3000.

Entry regulations

Information on US entry regulations is found at travel.state.gov.

Etiquette

New Yorkers have a reputation for being brusque and outspoken. It's a generalization, but not entirely unfounded. This is a fast-paced city with a hard-charging attitude. That said, you will find that most citizens are very helpful if you seek assistance. This is also an extraordinarily diverse city. And while New Yorkers are hardly paragons of universal brotherhood, they manage to get along in a sort of workaday fashion that keeps the city from flying apart at the seams.

Gay and lesbian

The traditional epicenter of New York's large gay community used to be Greenwich Village – the West Village in particular, on and around Christopher Street – but recently the center of gravity has shifted to Chelsea. Other popular neighborhoods are the East Village and Hell's Kitchen, in the 40s, west of the Theater District. Gay and lesbian travelers will find Manhattan a mostly tolerant and friendly place with a host of bars and clubs where gays congregate. Gay Pride Week in late June is celebrated with a big Fifth Avenue parade, and the annual flamboyant Halloween Parade in Greenwich Village brings thousands of spectators.

Useful resources

Lesbian, Gay, Bisexual and Transgender Community Center: 208 West 13th Street (at Seventh Avenue); tel: 212-620-7310; www.gay-center.org; Mon–Sat 9am–10pm, Sun 9am–9pm. This large and helpful organization offers services and events ranging from health education, counseling, and political action to parties.

The departure hall at Grand Central Station

Gay and Lesbian Hotline: tel: 212-989-0999; Mon–Fri 4pm–midnight, Sat noon–5pm. Provides information about all aspects of gay life in New York, from bars to legal counseling.

Gay & Lesbian Anti-Violence Project: 240 West 35th Street; tel: 212-714-1141; www.avp.org. Organization providing legal advocacy for victims of anti-gay violence.

Gay Men's Health Crisis: 446 West 33rd Street; tel: 212-367-1000; www.gmhc.org. This non-profit group assists people with HIV/AIDS.

Newspapers and magazines

Gay City News: gaycitynews.com. Covers local, national, and world news.

Next: www.nextmagazine.net. Dedicated to the best in gay entertainment in New York.

Time Out New York Magazine: www.timeout.com/newyork. Runs a large weekly listing of gay clubs and events.

H

Health and medical care

Medical services are extremely expensive. Purchase comprehensive travel insurance to cover any emergencies.

A source if you need non-emergency house calls is Doctors on Call: tel: 718-238-2100.

Emergency medical treatment

Bellevue Hospital: First Avenue and East 27th Street; tel: 212-562-4141.

Beth Israel Medical Center: First Avenue at 16th St; tel: 212-420-2000.

Lenox Hill Hospital: 77th Street and Park Avenue; tel: 212-434-2000.

Mount Sinai Hospital: Fifth Avenue and 100th Street; tel: 212-241-6500.

New York Presbyterian Hospital: 525 East 68th Street; tel: 212-746-5454.

New York Presbyterian Medical Center at Columbia University: 630 West 168th Street; tel: 212-305-2500.

NYU Medical Center: 550 First Avenue at 33rd Street; tel: 212-263-7300.

St Luke's-Roosevelt Hospital: 59th Street between Ninth and Tenth avenues; tel: 212-523-4000.

Hours and holidays

Business hours

Department stores and shops tend to stay open later, typically 10am to 8.30pm. Sunday hours are shorter, usually 11am to 6 or 7pm. Banks are normally open 9am to 3pm (although ATMs are everywhere), but increasingly they are opening as early as 8am and staying open until late afternoon or early evening.

Public holidays

The US has shifted most public holidays to the Monday closest to the actual dates, thereby creating a number of three-day weekends. Holidays that are observed no matter the day on which they fall are:

New Year's Day (January 1).

Independence Day (July 4).

Consulting the map in Central Park

Veterans' Day (November 11).
Christmas Day (December 25).
Other holidays are:
Martin Luther King Jr Day (third Mon in Jan).
President's Day (third Mon in Feb).
Memorial Day (last Mon in May).
Labor Day (first Mon in Sep).
Columbus Day (second Mon in Oct).
Election Day (first Tue in Nov).
Thanksgiving (fourth Thur in Nov).

I

Internet

Free public WiFi is available in Union Square, Bryant Park, Chelsea Market, South Street Seaport, the Winter Garden (World Financial Center), Lincoln Center Park, public libraries throughout Manhattan, and in numerous cafés and restaurants.

Most hotels provide WiFi (often at an additional fee) in their guest rooms, too. Email can be sent from the majority of FedEx Office branches or from computers at most public libraries.

L

Lost property

The chances of retrieving lost property are not high, but the occasional civic-minded individual may turn items in to the nearest police precinct. To inquire about items left on public transportation (subway and bus), tel: 212-712-4500; Mon, Tue,

Fri 8am–3.30pm, Wed, Thur 11am–6.30pm. Or call 311.

M

Maps

NYC & Co. has good maps at their visitor center and online at www.nycgo.com. Subway and bus maps are available at subway station booths, or from the New York City Transit Authority booth in Grand Central Terminal and the Long Island Rail Road information booth in Penn Station, as well as the MTA booth at the Times Square Visitors Center.

You can also download them from new.mta.info.

Media

Print

The *New York Times* and *Wall Street Journal* are both regarded as papers of national significance, and they are also strong on local issues. The *Times'* bulky Sunday edition has extensive coverage of local arts and entertainment.

Two papers compete for the tabloid market: the *New York Post* and the *Daily News*. There are two 'commuter' dailies distributed free in the mornings: *AM New York* and *Metro*. The free alternative weekly *Village Voice* has comprehensive listings and classified ads, as does the *New York Observer*. Local magazines with extensive event listings include *New York* and *Time Out New York*.

One–way street signs   *Little Italy decorations*

Radio
There are more than 70 radio stations in New York City. Some of the better stations with local news include:
WMYC: 93.9FM/820AM
WABC: 770AM
WCBS: 880AM
WINS: 1010AM
WBBR: 1130AM

Television
The three major networks – all with New York headquarters – are ABC (Channel 7, 47 West 66th Street; tel: 212-456-7777), CBS (Channel 2, 51 West 52nd Street; tel: 212-975-4321), and NBC (Channel 4, 30 Rockefeller Plaza; tel: 212-664-4444). Fox News has a national office at 1211 Sixth Avenue (tel: 212-556-2500) and a local studio (Channel 5, 205 East 67th Street; tel: 212-452-3983). CNN has offices at the Time Warner Center. Channel 13, the local Public Broadcasting Service (PBS) affiliate, has open studios at Lincoln Center. The other local stations are UPN (9) and CW (11).

Various cable companies offer hundreds of specialized cable and movie channels. Check newspaper listings for channel numbers.

With advance planning, it's possible to join the audience of a New York-based TV show, many of them shown overseas. Tickets are often free and sometimes distributed by lottery. For details, go to www.nycgo.com or see the website of your favorite program.

Money
Credit cards and ATMs
Cash advances on major credit and debit cards can be obtained from bank tellers and bank ATMs (automatic teller machines), which are marked with the corresponding stickers (ie Cirrus, Plus, Visa, MasterCard, American Express, etc.) Most of these charge a fee for withdrawing cash. Credit cards are accepted almost everywhere, although not all cards at all places.

Currency exchange
There are many outlets for exchanging currency and cashing travelers checks. These are accepted in most hotels and restaurants (as long as they are in dollars) and can be cashed at most banks. Some banks charge a fee for this service. Photo identification is required.

Travelex, a well-known source for currency exchange, has two convenient Midtown locations, tel: 800-287-7362; 1578 Broadway at 47th Street, tel: 212-265-6063; 1271 Broadway at 32nd Street, tel: 212-679-4365; and two Downtown offices, 29 Broadway, tel: 212-363-6206; and 30 Vesey Street, tel: 212-227-8156.

American Express has an office at 374 Park Avenue, tel: 212-421-8240 for selling and cashing travelers checks. Check www.amextravelresources.com for travel agencies that can also provide American Express

Times Square signs

travelers check services.

There is also an automated self-change kiosk at the Times Square Information Center at 1560 Broadway (between 46th and 47th streets).

Citibank offers exchange facilities at most branches. Tel: 800-285-3000.

Refunds

Department stores usually allow you to return merchandise up to 30 days after purchase for full credit. Boutiques are less accommodating; some allow store credit only, no returns on sale items, and no returns or exchanges after seven days.

P

Postal services

Manhattan's main post office is on Eighth Avenue between 31st and 33rd streets; it is open 24 hours a day. To locate post offices elsewhere in the five boroughs, call 800-275-8777 or go to www.usps.com.

R

Religion

New York is approximately 70 percent Christian, 11 percent Jewish, 1.5 percent Muslim, and 7.4 percent agnostic, with Buddhists, Hindus, and others also represented. Some 6,000 churches, synagogues, temples, and mosques can be found in the city's five boroughs.

Rest stops

When energy flags, New York has thoughtfully provided seating areas on Broadway between 42nd and 47th streets, at Herald Square between 33rd and 35th streets, and around Lincoln Center. Public restrooms are found in public parks but otherwise are in short supply in New York. Look for department stores, hotels, large book stores, or Starbucks coffee shops, which do have restrooms. In some cases you will have to request a key.

S

Security

Be prepared to pass through security checkpoints with metal detectors at such tourist attractions as the Statue of Liberty and Empire State Building.

Smoking

There is a no-smoking law in effect in virtually all New York City bars, restaurants, and offices. Be sure to request a smoking room if needed when booking a place to stay. The legal age to buy cigarettes is 18.

Street grid

In Midtown and Uptown Manhattan, avenues run north and south; streets run east and west. Even-numbered streets tend to have one-way eastbound traffic; odd-numbered streets,

Traffic in Chelsea

westbound traffic. Exceptions are 14th, 23rd, 57th, 72nd, 79th and 86th streets, which have two-way traffic and crosstown bus services. Most avenues are one-way, except for Park Avenue which has two-way traffic north of 44th Street, and Broadway north of 57th Street. The picture is more confusing in Greenwich Village and other Downtown neighborhoods, where most streets have names instead of numbers and run at all angles.

T

Taxis

Taxis, all metered, cruise the streets and must be hailed, although there are designated taxi stands at bus and train stations. Be sure to flag down an official yellow cab. The light on top is lit when the cab is available. The base rate on taxi fares is $2.50 upon entry plus 50¢ for every one-fifth of a mile (when the taxicab is traveling at 6 miles an hour or more) or 60 seconds (when not in motion). The flat rate for a taxi between JFK and Manhattan is $52 plus tolls. There is a $1 surcharge on all taxi rides from 4pm to 8pm on weekdays, and a 50¢ surcharge from 8pm to 6am.
24-hr taxi hotline: tel: 311

Water taxis

New York Water Taxis provide ferry service on the Hudson and East rivers. In addition to commuter services, water taxis offer hop-on-hop-off tours around the harbor on summer weekends and scenic tours. See www.ny watertaxi.com.

Telephone and faxes

Most Manhattan locations have a 212 area code, or the recently added 646. Cell phones can be 646 or 917. Brooklyn, Queens, Staten Island, and Bronx numbers are prefixed by 718 or the newer 347. The area code of the number being called must be used even within the city.

Toll-free calls are prefixed by 800, 866, 877, or 888.

Public telephones accepting credit cards are becoming scarce, but can still be found in centers such as Grand Central Terminal and Penn Station. Hotels usually add a hefty surcharge for phone calls. Telephone dialing cards, available at convenience stores and newsstands, are an inexpensive way to make calls.

Cell phones

If you are a foreign traveler and your cell phone plan doesn't include international service, consider purchasing a prepaid cell phone or SIM card, available at most electronic stores.

Fax

Most major hotels offer a fax service; faxes can also be sent from many copy and printing shops, as well as from the numerous branches of FedEx Office

stores, which offer computer access for a fee.

Useful numbers

International calls, dial 011 (the international access code), then the country code, city code, and local number.

Directory help, dial 555-1212 preceded by the area code you are calling from, or 411.

Non-emergency services

New York has a three-digit number to be dialed for information and non-emergency services. Calls to 311 are answered by a live operator 24 hours a day, seven days a week, and services are provided in over 170 languages. Operators are prepared to respond to a wide range of calls, including tourist inquiries, complaints about noise, queries about public transportation, and information about lost items.

Time zone

New York observes Eastern Standard Time (EST) and Eastern Daylight Time (EDT). This is usually five hours behind London, and always one hour ahead of Chicago, and three hours ahead of California.

Tipping

Most New Yorkers in the service industries (restaurants, hotels, transportation) regard tips as a God-given right, not just a pleasant gratuity. The fact is, many people rely on tips to make up for what are often poor hourly salaries. Therefore, unless service is truly horrendous, you can figure on tipping everyone from bellmen and porters (usually $1 a bag; or $2 if only one bag); to hotel doormen ($2 if they hail you a cab); hotel maids ($1–2 a day, left in your room when you check out), restroom attendants (at least 50¢), and room-service waiters (approximately 15 percent of the bill unless already added on).

In restaurants, an easy way to figure out the tip is to double the tax, which adds up to a little more than 16 percent (though 18–20 percent is becoming standard). In taxis, tip 15 percent of the total fare.

Tourist information

NYC & Company Visitors Information Center: 810 Seventh Avenue (between West 52nd and 53rd streets); tel: 212-484-1222, 800-NYC-VISIT; www.nycgo.com; Mon–Fri 8.30am–6pm, Sat–Sun 9am–5pm. The center offers brochures, maps, and information about hotels and attraction discounts. An information kiosk is at Broadway and Park Row at City Hall Park.

Times Square Museum Visitors Center: Seventh Avenue (between West 46th and 47th streets); tel: 212-452-5283; www.timessquarenyc.org; daily 8am–8pm. City info, plus Broadway show tickets.

Brooklyn Bridge

Transportation

Subways and buses

Subways and buses run 24 hours a day, less frequently (and some lines not at all) after midnight. Fares are payable by MetroCard pass (available at subway ticket booths), which allows free transfers between buses or buses and subways within two hours of use. Unlimited-ride passes for seven or 30 days are available.

Buses run on most avenues (except Park Avenue) as well as on the following cross-streets: Houston, 14th, 23rd, 34th, 42nd, 49th–50th, 57th, 66th, 79th, 86th, 96th, 116th, and 125th.

Subway shuttle trains cross town at 14th and 42nd streets. Queens lines N and R also cross from east to west in Manhattan. There is no north–south line east of Lexington Avenue or west of Eighth Avenue and Broadway.

For bus and subway information, call: 718-330-1234 or 511, or see www.mta.info.

PATH trains

PATH (Port Authority Trans Hudson) trains run under the Hudson River from Manhattan to Hoboken, Jersey City, and Newark in New Jersey. For information, call 800-234-PATH, or see www.panynj.gov/path.

Rail and bus stations

Long-distance and commuter trains arrive and depart from Manhattan's Grand Central Terminal at Park Avenue and 42nd Street, and Pennsylvania Station at Seventh Avenue and 33rd Street. For information on Amtrak, the national rail service, tel: 800-872-7245, www.amtrak.com.

The city's main bus terminal is Port Authority (Eighth Avenue between 40th and 42nd streets). The station sits on two subway lines and is serviced by long-distance bus companies (including Greyhound: tel: 800-231-2222; www.greyhound.com) and commuter lines. City buses stop outside.

Websites

www.newyork.citysearch.com for listings and reviews of current arts and entertainment events, as well as restaurants and shopping.

www.nyc.gov is the official site of the City of New York.

www.nycgo.com is the New York City tourism website, with information on hotels, restaurants, shopping, events, and promotions.

www.centralparknyc.org details what's on at and all about Central Park, including maps.

www.nypl.org is for everything you ever wanted to know about the New York Public Library. There's also an online information service.

Weights and measures

The US uses the imperial system.

BOOKS AND FILM

The year 1888, when writer William Dean Howells abandoned Boston for the Big Apple, is often seen as the moment when New York moved into the lead of America's literary enterprise. And so it remains. The industry nurtured such major talents as Henry James and Edith Wharton, who forged an old New York mystique later augmented by waves of writers coming from other cultures – Jewish, Irish, African-American, Italian, and more.

When it comes to movies, there's something about New York that loves the camera. From all those wide-angle sweeps up, down, and across the city's imposing skyscrapers to the down-and-dirty peeks at what lies beneath, moviemakers have found Gotham an irresistible backdrop.

Books

History

The Gangs of New York: An Informal History of the Underworld by Herbert Asbury. The book on which the Martin Scorsese film is based takes readers on a journey to a bygone New York, when violent gangs ruled the Five Points near present-day City Hall.

Gotham: A History of New York to 1898 by Mike Wallace and Edwin G. Burrows. Pulitzer Prize-winning narrative about the city's early years; in-depth, with an emphasis on some of its characters.

How the Other Half Lives by Jacob Riis. Groundbreaking account of the squalid tenements and sweatshops of the 19th century.

New York: The Story of a Great City edited by Sarah Henry. A concise, visual history of the city as compiled by the Museum of the City of New York.

Writing New York: A Literary Anthology edited by Philip Lopate. Observations about life in New York by such literary folk as Henry David Thoreau, Walt Whitman, Maxim Gorky, and F. Scott Fitzgerald.

Contemporary non-fiction

New York Stories: The Best of the City Section of the New York Times edited by Constance Rosenblum. An anthology of essays about city life from the Times.

Sex and the City by Candace Bushnell. These sex columns from the New York Observer served as the inspiration for the popular TV series.

Still Life in Harlem by Eddy L. Harris. An autobiographical take on this storied African-American neighborhood.

Fiction

The Age of Innocence by Edith Wharton. A portrait of upper-crust New York in the 19th century.

The Bonfire of the Vanities by Tom Wolfe. Satirical novel set in the New York of the 1980s.

Gene Hackman takes notes in 'The French Connection'

Bright Lights, Big City by Jay McInerney. Novel set in yuppie New York during the cocaine-saturated 1980s by one of the period's rising literary stars.

Wonderful Town: New York Stories from The New Yorker edited by David Remnick. Work by Philip Roth, John Cheever, Susan Sontag, and others are collected in this anthology of short stories from the venerable literary magazine.

Films

Here's just a short selection of iconic New York movies.

Miracle on 34th Street, 1947. A classic Christmas story. The 1994 remake is even more sugary than the original, but Richard Attenborough makes a good Santa Claus.

Breakfast at Tiffany's, 1961. Audrey Hepburn and George Peppard search for love, diamonds, and breakfast in a bittersweet tale based (with some huge liberties taken) on the Truman Capote novel.

West Side Story, 1961. Romeo and Juliet are transported to Hell's Kitchen with irresistible energy in this near-definitive New York musical by Leonard Bernstein and Stephen Sondheim.

Midnight Cowboy, 1969. Dustin Hoffman and Jon Voight are down-on-their-luck hustlers in this vivid evocation of 1960s street life.

The French Connection, 1971. A riveting performance by Gene Hackman as cop Popeye Doyle, and the daddy of all New York car chases.

Taxi Driver, 1976. Martin Scorsese directs Robert De Niro as a psychotic cabbie who tries to save a child prostitute played by Jodie Foster.

Saturday Night Fever, 1977. John Travolta is a dancing fool in this portrait of the 1970s suburban disco scene, with music by the Bee Gees that just stays in your head.

Manhattan, 1978. Woody Allen's ode to his hometown and his own neuroses is shot in black and white and stars Allen, Diane Keaton, and Meryl Streep.

Wall Street, 1987. 'Greed is good,' declares Michael Douglas in this Oliver Stone film, neatly summing up the excesses of the go-go 1980s.

Do the Right Thing, 1989. Spike Lee riffs on racial tensions in Brooklyn's Bedford-Stuyvesant neighborhood.

When Harry Met Sally, 1989. The city looks fantastic in this romantic comedy about friendship and love, with Meg Ryan and Billy Crystal.

Basquiat, 1996. A film by Julian Schnabel about Brooklyn-born graffiti artist Jean-Michel Basquiat, who made a big splash in the Downtown art scene of the 1980s.

Nick and Norah's Infinite Playlist, 2008. A coming-of-age romantic comedy in the world of indie rock which takes place in one evening mostly in the Lower East Side and East Village.

The Avengers, 2012. The metropolis ends up a little worse-for-wear after this superhero extravaganza.

ABOUT THIS BOOK

This *Explore Guide* has been produced by the editors of Insight Guides, whose books have set the standard for visual travel guides since 1970. With top-quality photography and authoritative recommendations, these guidebooks bring you the very best routes and itineraries in the world's most exciting destinations.

BEST ROUTES

The routes in the book provide something to suit all budgets, tastes and trip lengths. As well as covering the destination's many classic attractions, the itineraries track lesser-known sights and embrace a range of interests, so whether you are an art fan, a gourmet, a history buff or have kids to entertain, you will find an option to suit.

We recommend reading the whole of a route before setting out. This should help you to familiarise yourself with it and enable you to plan where to stop for refreshments – options are shown in the 'Food and Drink' box at the end of each tour.

For our pick of the tours by theme, consult Recommended Routes for… (see pages 4–5).

INTRODUCTION

The routes are set in context by this introductory section, giving an overview of the destination to set the scene, plus background information on food and drink, shopping and more, while a succinct history timeline highlights the key events over the centuries.

DIRECTORY

Also supporting the routes is a Directory chapter, with a clearly organised A–Z of practical information, our pick of where to stay while you are there and select restaurant listings; these eateries complement the more low-key cafés and restaurants that feature within the routes and are intended to offer a wider choice for evening dining. Also included here are select nightlife listings and our recommendations for books and films about the destination.

ABOUT THE AUTHORS

Writer Aaron Starmer has spent the last twelve years exploring the streets, parks, and restaurants of New York City. He has written and contributed to numerous guidebooks, including *Insight City Guide New York*, and is the author of two novels for young people.

This book draws on original content by Eleanor Berman and John Gattuso, as well as Edward A. Jardim, William Scheller, Kathy Novak, and Divya Symmers.

CONTACTING EDITORS

We would appreciate it if readers would alert us to errors or outdated information by writing to us at insight@apaguide.co.uk or APA Publications, PO Box 7910, London SE1 1WE, UK.

CREDITS

Explore New York

Contributors: Aaron Starmer, Eleanor Berman, John Gattuso

Commissioning Editor: Sarah Clark

Series Editor: Sarah Clark

Art Editor: Tom Smyth

Map Production: Berndtson & Berndtson, updated by Apa Cartography Department

Production: Tynan Dean and Rebeka Davies

Photo credits: Ace Hotels 107; Alamy 20, 21, 56, 123, 136; AWL Images 2/3T, 24/25T; Bigstock 70, 86/87, 98/99; Britta Jaschinski/Apa 2MC, 18, 19L, 26/27, 27L, 29, 60, 62, 62/63, 63L, 64, 66L, 78/79, 79L, 85, 86, 94, 95, 99, 120; Casablanca Hotel 102; Daniel 14, 114/115, 115L; Dreamstime 2MR, 4TL, 4MC, 9L, 26, 34, 38L, 38/39, 46, 47L, 48, 48/49, 49L, 50, 50/51, 55L, 59, 60/61, 76L, 76/77, 90, 92/93, 96, 122, 124, 128/129; Fotolia 2MR, 6ML, 24MC, 61L, 68/69, 116/117; Getty Images 4ML, 125L, 137; Gramercy Tavern 100ML; Hotel on Rivington 110/111; iStock 1, 2MC, 2ML, 5MR, 5M, 5MR, 8T, 8/9, 24ML, 24ML, 24MR, 30, 31L, 32, 34/35, 35L, 36, 40/41, 42L, 42/43, 46/47, 52, 58, 71, 74, 81, 82, 96/97, 97L, 98L, 100MR, 100/101T; JC Smith/Four Seasons 112/113, 113L; K Niwa/Tenement Museum 88/89; Leonardo 100MC, 100MR, 103, 104, 104/105, 105L, 108, 109, 114; Mary Evans 22, 23; M Bodycomb/The Frick Collection 57; Nobu 121; Nowitz Photography/Apa 2ML, 4BC, 6ML, 6MC, 6MC, 6MR, 6/7T, 8B, 10, 10/11, 11L, 12T, 12B, 13, 15, 16T, 16B, 17, 18/19, 24MR, 24MC, 28, 30/31, 33, 43, 44, 51L, 53, 54, 54/55, 65, 66/67, 67, 72, 73, 75, 77, 78, 80, 83, 84, 87L, 88, 90/91, 91L, 100MC, 118, 119, 124/125, 126, 126/127, 127L, 130, 130/131, 131L, 132, 133, 134/135; NYC Ballet 5T; Robert Harding 37, 39; Sony 45; Starwood Hotels 106, 112

Cover credits: Front Cover Main *Travel Pictures*; Front Cover BL *iStockphoto;* Back Cover: (Left) Manhattan *iStockphoto* (Right): Central Park *Dreamstime*

Printed by CTPS – China

First Edition 2014

DISTRIBUTION

Worldwide
APA Publications GmbH & Co. Verlag KG (Singapore branch)
7030 Ang Mo Kio Ave 5, 08-65 Northstar @ AMK, Singapore 569880
Email: apasin@singnet.com.sg

UK and Ireland
Dorling Kindersley Ltd (a Penguin Company)
80 Strand, London, WC2R 0RL, UK
Email: customerservice@uk.dk.com

US
Ingram Publisher Services
One Ingram Blvd, PO Box 3006, La Vergne, TN 37086-1986
Email: ips@ingramcontent.com

Australia
Universal Publishers
PO Box 307, St. Leonards NSW 1590
Email: sales@universalpublishers.com.au

New Zealand
Brown Knows Publications
11 Artesia Close, Shamrock Park, Auckland, New Zealand 2016
Email: sales@brownknows.co.nz

INDEX

MAP LEGEND

●   Start of tour

➝   Tour & route direction

❶   Recommended sight

❷   Recommended
    restaurant/café

★   Place of interest

ⓘ   Tourist information

Ⓜ   Subway station

𝟏   Statue/monument

✉   Main post office

🚌   Main bus station

-----   Ferry route

– – –   National park boundry

·– – –   District boundary

   Park

   Important building

   Hotel

   Transport hub

   Shopping / mall

   Pedestrian area

   Urban area

   Marsh

INSIGHT GUIDES

INSPIRING YOUR NEXT ADVENTURE

Insight Guides offers you a range of travel guides to match your needs. Whether you are looking for inspiration for planning a trip, cultural information, walks and tours, great listings, or practical advice, we have a product to suit you.

www.insightguides.com